Recollections
of an
Occasional Attorney

To M: an old friend
John Iglehart

Francis N. Iglehart

American Literary Press, Inc.
Five Star Special Edition
Baltimore, Maryland

Recollections of an Occasional Attorney

Library of Congress
Cataloging-in-Publication Data
ISBN 1-56167-862-7

Library of Congress Card Catalog Number:
2004094094

Published by

American Literary Press, Inc.
Five Star Special Edition
8019 Belair Road, Suite 10
Baltimore, Maryland 21236

Manufactured in the United States of America

For Raz Parker and the
rest of the crew

TABLE OF CONTENTS

PREFACE

Several years ago, I was moved to commit to paper my memory of service as an infantryman in World War II. It had a good reception among friends and strangers. I found that writing provided a good catharsis for events of the past.

As I thought back on other events in my life, it seemed that there were a lot of stories to tell, some humorous, some tragic, but that the past was worthy of reconstruction within my limited ability to be the reconstructor. By profession, I am a lawyer, but it should be quite apparent from what follows that my interests went far beyond the "dry as dust" tomes of the law, and that I was truly an "occasional" attorney.

I have given a partial genealogy as the only certain readers of the book will be some family members. Other readers might want to skip forward to Chapter 2 at page 15. Having embarked on this endeavor, one thing that stands out is how our sense of time changes once we have gone into the past. For example, many of the relatives referred to in the first chapter lived almost a century, spanning enormous changes taking place in our country, financially and technologically. The Civil War that once appeared so distant in time now seems like it happened "only yesterday." Remote ancestors now seem much closer, and one's whole perspective on the past changes.

RECOLLECTIONS OF AN OCCASIONAL ATTORNEY

CHAPTER 1
FORBEARS

On the Paternal Side

There are various fanciful legends about the origin of the name Iglehart. One has a distant ancestor taking the heart of the emperor to the Holy Land during one of the last Crusades, hence the name. Anyone with a rudimentary knowledge of the German language would know that the word for "heart" is "herz." In fact, the name Iglehart could be the combination of the word "Igle," which is the name for badger, with "hart," meaning tough as a badger; not a bad sobriquet. Another story has a less distant ancestor being forced to flee from Saxony in the late 1600s due to a dispute with an elector of the Holy Roman Empire and fleeing to England where he was asked to leave again. One version has him resettling near Armagh in Ireland and marrying an Irish lady. However, no link to any of these people can be found through searching backwards in current genealogical records.

A systematic search on the paternal side by Robert W. Barnes, a professional genealogist, only takes us back as far as Jacob Ingleheart, who witnessed a Will of one Robert Wheeler of Prince George's County in 1740. In 1753, Jacob married Jane Perry of

Prince George's County. They had 10 children, including James Iglehart, who was born in 1752 and died at his home in Anne Arundel County in 1825.

James married Ann Sellman in 1788. Some idea of James' standing in the community can be gathered from the probate inventory for his estate, which was opened in 1825. He left to son, John, half of his farm and to his son, Thomas, the other half along with four Negro men, one Negro woman, and the choice of four horses, six oxen, five milk cows, and twenty sheep. Son, James, was to have 23 shares of stock in the Farmer's Bank of Maryland and the choice of a Negro boy. Each grandchild was to have a Negro slave.

The second James Iglehart, son of James and Ann Sellman Iglehart, was born in 1790 and died in Annapolis in 1874, having married Rachel Ann Harwood in 1822. A Census record in 1850 shows that John Iglehart (probably an erroneous reading for James), merchant, lived in Annapolis owning $15,000 worth of real estate. Living with him were Mrs. Waddle, age 26 (presumably his daughter Ann); J.I. Waddle, age 23, U.S. Navy (presumably his son-in-law); H. Iglehart, age 21, lawyer; James Jr., age 18, student; William age 16, student; O.L., age 13, student; and a Miss E. Mills, age 60 – an intriguing scrap of information from the past which will be discussed at greater length later herein.

James and Rachel Harwood Iglehart were the parents of Ann, born in 1824, who married James Iredell Waddell of North

Carolina in 1848. They were the parents of six other children, including James Iglehart III, who was wounded at Culp's Hill in the battle of Gettysburg in July 1863 in the 2nd Maryland Confederate Regiment, and died several days later. In 1855, he had married Sarah (Sally) Waddell in North Carolina, sister of James Iredell Waddell. Sarah was born in 1830, the daughter of Francis Nash and Elizabeth E. Moore Waddell. James and Sarah were the parents of Charles Iredell Iglehart, born in 1856, his mother having died three years later. The death of James III from wounds received at Gettysburg left Charles Iredell effectively an orphan. Charles died at Morgantown, North Carolina in 1915 and is buried in Annapolis near his brother-in-law, James Iredell Waddell, commander of the Confederate raider, Shenandoah in the last year of the Civil War.

In 1880, Charles Iredell Iglehart married Anna Calhoun Robinson, born in 1858, who died in 1938. She was the great-granddaughter of James Calhoun, the first mayor of Baltimore. She was also the granddaughter of Alexander C. Robinson, who married Angelica Peale, the daughter of Charles Wilson Peale, the eminent artist and painter of George Washington. At the time of her death, she was living with her sister, Louisa Hall Robinson and was survived by a son, Francis N. Iglehart and seven grandchildren: Lucy James Howard, Angelica Peale Allan, Elizabeth Blair, Francis N. Iglehart, Jr., Alice W. Iglehart, Anne Calhoun

Iglehart, and Iredell W. Iglehart, Jr. She and Charles Iredell Iglehart were also parents of Iredell W. Iglehart, born in 1885, who died in 1934, father of cousin Idy, and grandfather of Dr. Iredell Iglehart. He married Alice Whitridge and they were parents of Alice Bowie Whitridge, Iredell Waddell Iglehart, Jr., and Anne Calhoun Sommers.

Francis N. Iglehart, son of Charles Iredell and Anna Calhoun Robinson Iglehart, was born in 1881 in Baltimore and married Lucy James Cook in 1907 in her mother's St. Paul Street apartment in Baltimore. She was born in 1882, the daughter of Captain George Hamilton Cook, USA. Francis Nash Iglehart was a member of the Class of 1903 at Johns Hopkins University and was a real estate broker for most of his active career, being President of F.N. Iglehart & Co. He was also for a time a director of the Dun & Bradstreet Corp.

This establishes the bare bones of the genealogy on the paternal side, but it is worth having commentary on some of the persons listed here. It should be obvious from the probate records for the first James Iglehart that the family had a Southern orientation, not only because they lived in Anne Arundel County, but by economic circumstance through the ownership of slaves. Thus it is not surprising that our great-grandfather, James III, fought with the South serving in the 2nd Maryland Infantry CSA at Gettysburg. He was married to the sister of the Waddell who commanded the

4

Shenandoah, who in turn married his sister, Ann. Since Capt. Waddell sank 26 Northern whaling ships in the Bering Straits in August 1865, well after the end of the war, he prudently brought his ship around the Horn all the way to England and went into exile with Ann. Eventually some ten (10) years after the war, he received a pardon and settled in Annapolis where he once lived with his young bride in her family home and was made commander of the Maryland Tidewater Fisheries Commission, dying in 1886. An impressive obelisk was erected in St. Anne's cemetery commemorating his Confederate naval career, and the church itself was the recipient of a handsome lectern in the form of a brass eagle in his memory purchased with private donations.

Family Oral History

We now get into a realm that is somewhat uncertain and conjectural, mainly oral history. As children we were told, presumably by our mother, that grandfather Charles Iredell Iglehart was a noted amateur gymnast, who suffered a severe injury on the horizontal bar in the gymnasium where he was working out, doing the giant swing, when the bar broke, hurling him against a brick wall and fracturing his skull. The result of this serious injury was a lifetime of incapacity, extreme headaches, and resort to the bottle. Grandmother Iglehart, who was reputedly very straight-laced, refused to talk about him so that we never knew what he had done for a living or anything else about him other than that he had been in a sanitorium in North Carolina for many years; so our grandfather remained a shadowy figure for us. For me, the mental image that was conjured up was a scene in a gym with a horizontal bar breaking under the stress of a giant swing performed by a muscular athlete, who was never "right" from that date forward. He left us in 1915 to join the Confederate ancestor group in St. Anne's Cemetery in Annapolis.

My father, Francis Nash Iglehart, must have inherited some of the athletic prowess and bent of Charles as evidenced by a photograph taken of him stripped to the waist, flexing his biceps of which he must have been quite proud. In college, he played ice hockey and cricket, which had become quite the thing for turn of the century youth in the Baltimore area. In later years, he was an avid tennis player and golfer, often playing 36 holes on a Saturday in the pre-golf cart era. My earliest memory of him is his coming back perspiring from a three mile jog down Greenspring Avenue to Hillside Road where the local railroad station was then located, followed up by a workout with 5 lb. dumbbells, an ice cold bath, and a heavy dose of sauerkraut juice – a loathsome concoction. He made me sleep outside on a "sleeping porch" under a buffalo robe during the winter and I emulated him to the extent of taking ice cold baths myself, which apparently was a late-Victorian fad, but I was never able to handle the sauerkraut juice.

Conversely, my mother, born Lucy James Cook, was physically quite frail, afflicted with asthma all of her life with frequent trips to the hospital during the high pollen season. She was very musical, played the piano, loved to dance, very well read, but otherwise the total opposite of my father. Many years later, taking a course in German at Princeton, I was introduced to Thomas Mann, whose theory that physical frailty went with intellectuality and the creative side in contrast to the physically robust burgher type gripped my imagination. I read the short story "Der Bajazzo" as a prelude to "Buddenbrooks," and I realized with a shock that Mann depicted my parents, though possibly in a somewhat exaggerated form. However, I am getting ahead of my story which should now turn to the maternal side of the family.

On the Maternal Side

The James Family

When we turn to the maternal side of the Iglehart family, we find that our focus shifts northward to Lockport, New York, Ohio, and Missouri and a Northern political orientation. The Cooks were from Lockport, New York, but the James family were from Chillicothe, Ohio and St. James, Missouri. Let us deal with the James side first because an uncle's Will and a fortuitous set of circumstances made a great difference in the lives of the family on this side as we shall see later on.

For this information about the James family, I am indebted to Jean Genet, whose biography of cousin Lucy Wortham James was published by the James Foundation, created in her Will when she died in 1938. A James ancestor is reputed to have been an iron master who settled in Maryland in the 1640s. His descendant, Thomas James, set out for the west on foot in 1797 as a 21 year old settling first in the new town of Chillicothe, Ohio, then capital of the Northwest Territory. A merchant, he dealt in practically everything, bartering with the Indians with iron for furs and ginseng, which he began shipping in large quantities to China. He made friends with General Massie, in charge of the land grant surveys for the Territory and married his sister, going into business partnership with the General. Both men were interested in mining and by 1816 were operating iron furnaces making nails, stoves, and plow shares. After his first wife died, he married Jane Claypoole, the daughter of a banker from Philadelphia.

One day in 1825, Thomas was visited by a delegation of Shawnee Indians. His visitors offered to show him the source of their red paint and this resulted in finding an ideal place for a future ironworks in the Ozark foothills with abundant water and iron ore nearby. By 1829, the ironworks were in production and soon doing a booming business among the pioneers settling in and passing through Missouri. The name of the location of the ironworks was Maramec, a corruption of an Indian word. In 1843, Thomas and Jane's son, William, went out from Chillocothe to manage the ironworks. When William arrived in Maramec, he had with him his young bride, Lucy Ann Dun, sister of Robert G. Dun, later the founder of Dun & Bradstreet.

The Civil War put a premium on Maramec Iron, but as the war drew to a close, William James made a major miscalculation, refusing to modernize the works and use the blast furnace techniques that were being used elsewhere. Rather than rolling the iron in bulk, it was hammered and extremely costly compared with iron from the new rolling mills. The ultimate result was bankruptcy. While William James was going into financial ruin, his brother-in-law, Robert Graham Dun, had founded the predecessor of Dun & Bradstreet, which was the beginning of a long success story. Generous to a fault, he helped William James by making him supervisor of a Colorado silver mine. Robert G. Dun ("Uncle Bob") had no children and when he died in 1900 at the age of 74, his Will provided that his entire residuary estate would go to the children of his sisters, Lucy Dun James and Elizabeth Dun Douglas, after providing income for life for his wife. His residuary estate apparently consisted of thousands of shares of Dun & Bradstreet which thereby passed in part to Jane James, our grandmother, who married George Hamilton Cook. She died in 1932 leaving three daughters, Lucy James Cook, my mother, born in 1882 who died in 1959, aunt Jane James Cook, born in 1885 who died in 1944, and Frances Swayne Cook, born in 1887, who died in 1962.

Grandmother Cook qualified as one of the residuary legatees. At the time of her death in 1932, the Dun & Bradstreet stock was worth very little but ultimately became the source of the family's fortune. Part of the family oral history is that our father, Francis Nash Iglehart, was serving on the company board and insisted that the stock not be sold by grandmother's Executors despite its extremely low value, and his advice was followed.

The Cook Connection

This information is extracted from my Aunt Jane Cook's massive and beautifully bound work on the history of the James and Cook families. Walter Cook, an ancestral pioneer, settled in the colony of Massachusetts Bay as early as 1643. A descendant, Amasa Cook, was born in 1772 in Rhode Island and died in 1843. Colonel Elliott Wilkinson Cook was a son of Amasa Cook and Mary Wilkinson Cook, born in 1818 in Rhode Island. In 1837, he moved to Lockport, New York with his mother and became by vocation a gun maker with an avocation for big game hunting in Canada, Michigan, and Illinois. He was a major in the New York state militia and in 1845 was appointed inspector of a brigade; raised a regiment for the Mexican war but did not go. In 1849, he went to California by way of the isthmus of Panama as treasurer of the Niagara and California Mining Company, remaining in the west for one year.

Major Cook answered Lincoln's call for volunteers in the Spring of 1861, served as Captain, Major, and Lieutenant Colonel of the 28th New York Volunteers from Niagara County. At the battle of Cedar Mountain, he was captured and confined for six weeks in Libby Prison. While in command of a regiment at the battle of Chancellorsville, he was again captured and for a second time confined in Libby Prison, but his luck held and he survived confinement.

In August 1864, he went to Tennessee for the purpose of recruiting Union sympathizers. He died in 1877 at Riverside, California where he had gone in hope of regaining his health. He had been married in 1842 to Malvina Louisa Littlefield. Their son, George Hamilton Cook, was born in 1846 in Lockport. At the age of 17 in 1864, he was commissioned 1st Lieutenant of volunteers and assigned to a "colored" unit, and was present in 1865 at the fall of Richmond. He was recommissioned in the regular Army in 1867 as 2nd Lieutenant, and in 1873 received the rank of 1st Lieutenant being stationed in Little Rock, Fort Brown, Texas, Fort

Leavenworth, and Fort Union, New Mexico, where he held the post of Captain and Assistant Quartermaster and where his daughter, Lucy James Cook, was born in 1882. He had married Jane James in 1881 at St. James, Missouri. He died in 1889 at Fort Slocum, New York. They had two daughters in addition to Lucy; Jane James Cook born in 1885, who never married, died in 1944, and Frances Swayne Cook, born in 1887, who died in 1962. In later years, my mother, Lucy, told us of seeing Apache prisoners being brought in to the stockade at Fort Union. She married Francis Nash Iglehart in 1907. He had attended Johns Hopkins University, was in the real estate business, served as a Captain in the U.S. Army Air Service during World War I. They had four children, Lucy James Iglehart, born in 1908, who died in 1990, married to Dr. John Eager Howard in 1928; Angelica Peale Iglehart, born in 1912, who died in 2002, married to Dr. Warde B. Allan in 1932; Elizabeth Graham Iglehart, born in 1917, who died in 2001, married Edward McCormick Blair of Chicago in 1942; and a son, Francis N. Iglehart, Jr., born in 1925, and married Harriet Austen Stokes in 1947. Dr. Howard was a direct descendant of the John Eager Howard, renowned as one of Maryland's Revolutionary War heroes. In his medical career, he pioneered in the treatment of kidney disease and its relationship to high blood pressure, and was eventually appointed as a full professor at the Johns Hopkins Medical School. Dr. Allan was a

12

native of Calgary and a graduate of McGill University. A distinguished internist, he taught first-year students at Hopkins. Edward Blair became the senior partner in the Chicago investment banking firm of William Blair & Sons.

The Iglehart family home was the Ivy Hill property at the corner of Greenspring Avenue and Valley Road, the title to which was taken by Lucy Cook Iglehart in 1913. Grandmother Cook took title to the Ledger Hill property on the west side of Greenspring Avenue in 1919. Waverly next to it became the Howard family home in 1932. Before Dr. Allan became a practicing physician, the Allans lived on McElderry Street near Hopkins hospital during his residency and later moved to Glen Oak, for many years their family home next to the Greenspring Valley Club golf course. The Blairs, of course, lived in Lake Bluff, Illinois after World War II.

Additional Oral History

My parents are supposed to have met at a skating party when a member of the group fell through the ice and was rescued by my father, who impressed all who were there by his bold action. His military career began with his service in the 110th Maryland National Guard Field Artillery battalion, which was activated at the time of Pancho Villa's incursion across the Mexican border. However, the 110th did not go there, but trained in a place called Tobyanna,

Pennsylvania where my father, a business man then in his mid-30s, eventually made Corporal, though he did not relish the job of applying Glover's mange cure to the battery horses which led to an embarrassing episode when he was invited out by a local lady for dinner nearby on a warm August evening when the odor of mange cure permeated the dining room. Convinced the 110th would never get overseas to France, my father enlisted in the Air Corps, was trained at Love Field, Texas and stationed at Berkeley, California where he was an assistant ground commandant. Apparently he did not have very good skills as a pilot, and was assigned to ground duty. He may have had a role in future military history by passing a young pilot cadet who flunked the Morse Code examination. That young student was Jimmy Doolittle. From Berkeley, my father was sent to France and became assistant commandant at the Toul airfield where Hobey Baker had his fatal crash after the Armistice was signed. The author's own military service in World War II has been memorialized in the small book "The Short Life of the ASTP" recounting his experiences in the savage fighting in the Battle of the Bulge and his escape from sudden death any number of times.

CHAPTER 2
PERSONAL HISTORY

The author was born on February 21, 1925 in the Woman's Hospital of Baltimore. The youngest of four children with older sisters, the youngest being seven years his senior. His mother, the former Lucy James Cook, was 42 years of age and afflicted with severe asthma. Childbirth under those circumstances seems like a minor miracle. For an only son it posed the question "What was I to do with my life?"

The earliest memories are of home at Ivy Hill which seems like an enchanted place, though it was an ordinary summer home built shortly after the Civil War and not intended for round-year use. There was a furnace fueled by anthracite coal forced into the furnace by a contraption called an "iron fireman." There was a wrap-around porch on three sides of the house which provided a great racecourse for tricycles and bicycles. It was the age when the middle class had servants – it being important to maintain appearances. Ivy Hill had a cook, an upstairs maid, and at times, a butler. Then there was a chauffeur, two gardeners who lived in houses on the property and a stableman otherwise known as a groom. The size of the staff did not seem unusual for many homes in the Greenspring Valley were similarly staffed.

To the immediate east was the Wickes' property known as Wickecliff, now Maryvale school. The house itself was a reconstituted 16th century English castle that had been moved to the States and rebuilt stone by stone. Mrs. Wickes was the daughter of Otto Young from Chicago, who had founded the first grocery store chain. Dr. Wickes was a physician originally from the Eastern Shore of Maryland who had the good fortune to marry Mrs. Wickes.

Immediately to the east of Wickecliff was the Brewster property known as Fernwood inhabited by Mrs. Wickes' daughter, Ottolie, and her husband, Daniel Baugh Brewster, who had served in the Marine Corps in World War I and reputedly had been gassed. They were the parents of Daniel Jr., many years later a United States Senator and Marine Corps hero in World War II. Then there were his younger brothers, Andre, who is my age, later Walter and a sister, Catherine.

One would assume with so many servants that the Brewster boys and I would have led a very pampered, sheltered life. It was to a certain extent, but we were allowed to roam pretty freely around the three properties, fishing, catching snapping turtles, squirrel hunting with 22s, and endangering ourselves and others near us as we approached the 4th of July.

My father bought me a pair of beagles, a dog and a bitch, and the Brewsters had some too. Eventually we formed a pack with those hounds and some that the Edward Murray family had. Our stable man/groom,

Ellwood Boblitz, a former whipper-in at the Greenspring Valley Hunt Club, acted as huntsman with horn and all. We had formal meets on Sundays and the highlight of the year was when we released an imported Kansas jackrabbit that meant many hours of looking for lost hounds, strewn about the countryside. The beagle pack introduced us to night hunting too and we would sit on the laurel-covered hillside facing towards to the Wickes estate with the Dipping Pond Run gurgling nearby, listening to the hounds running gray foxes as often as rabbits knowing that the fox would eventually go up a tree. It was a way to learn the voice of every hound in the pack. When I read the Voice of Bugle Ann, I knew that I had been there too.

It was an outdoors existence and we had far more freedom than kids of the same age have today. In addition to the squirrel hunting, fishing, and beagling, there was foxhunting which I was introduced to at the age of 8 when my father put me on a 17-hand, half-bred, western horse named Colorado then aged 18 or 19, who had carried my sisters safely in earlier years. A noble steed, he is now buried with a marker in what was the pasture field on the south side of Valley Road. In spite of being sent away to boarding school at the age of 13, these activities continued during school vacation times, though adolescence began to promote other interests as well.

For me, school consisted of two years at Calvert School where my clearest memory is being made to sit on a stool with a dunce cap because I could not read the words on the blackboard being nearsighted. Then followed five years at Gilman School. Only one fellow student in our class was for Roosevelt in 1936, Edward Stettinius, whose uncle was Secretary of State under FDR. Often driven to school by a chauffeur, we would lean out the car windows and shout insults at WPA workers digging ditches for pipelines on Lake Avenue.

For reasons best surmised at, a group of us were pulled out of Gilman and sent to St. Paul's in Concord, NH. Dan Brewster, his brother Andre, Tim Lanahan, later killed in action in World War II, Brent Keyser, and Donald Culver. We arrived at St. Paul's after the death of the legendary rector, Dr. Drury. We also arrived just at the time the 1938 hurricane swept up the Merrimac River valley felling thousands of trees. I can still remember looking at slate tile being ripped off the roofs of the buildings and flying through the air. Except for Dan, who was a year ahead of us, we were in the Second Form, obliged to wear starched-stiff collars for the evening meal. Chapel was obligatory every morning and twice on Sunday with an Evensong service. Athletics were also almost obligatory. Those who opted out were assigned to something called the grub squad which shoveled coal at the school power plant. The school was organized into three clubs – Ishmian, Delphians and Old Hundreds, so there was plenty of intramural contests. Rowing on nearby Turkey Lake was between the Halcyon and Shattuck crews.

I played club football and tried hockey in the Winter, but my skating technique was not sufficient to place me higher than a lower-club team; so some of us took up boxing coached by a legendary ex-flyweight professional named Dick Whalen. I caught too many "crabs" in the first boat I tried to row in, and took up track in the Spring running primarily the mile and 880.

Tim Lanahan was the son of one of my father's oldest friends. His estate, Long Crandon off of Dulaney Valley Road later became the site of the Archdiocese retirement home, Stella Maris. Tim's older brothers, Wallace Jr. and Jack, had preceded him at St. Paul's and I am sure Mr. Lanahan was influential in persuading my father to send me to St. Paul's. Tim became President of the Sixth Form in our senior year, and, surprisingly, Andre Brewster was elected Vice President despite the lack of geographical diversity. With Adonis-like good looks, Tim was a true scholar/athlete. He played first base on the Delphian team in the Spring and I was chagrined when Ronnie Clark, our track coach, detailed him to run the mile against the local high school. His time was considerably better than mine. In World War II, Tim went the ASTP route, which I will explain about later, and was killed as a rifleman crossing a bridge near Saarlautern in the 95th Division, part of Patton's Third Army. My mother was concerned about my reaction to news of his death and withheld the information from me until after the war was over. Wallace Jr. was in the 82nd Airborne and Jack, who was fighting semi-professionally coached by Dick Whalen, later married Scotty Fitzgerald after serving in the Navy on Gene Tunney's physical fitness staff. My father and Mr. Lanahan Sr. went to see him fight in places like Trenton and the Steelworker's Hall in East Baltimore. Tim idolized Jack and had a blownup photograph of him in the ring hanging in his room at school.

Academically we were given a choice of a Classical route taking Greek and Latin, modern languages consisting of French and German instruction, or a Scientific course which even in the Third Form gave us a curriculum equivalent to college freshman anatomy and physiology with a remarkable instructor named McConnell, who was a failed medical school student. In addition to dissecting frogs and cats, McConnell, had us doing book reports on such works as *"Designs in Scarlet"* to give us instruction in the dangers of venereal disease. We worked hard and discipline was omni-present, unlike the school today. I can remember sitting around in a group in what was called Middle House on December 7, 1941 hearing about Pearl Harbor on the radio. Everyone was ready to volunteer. Some, remarkably, talked about going into submarines which didn't particularly appeal to me. By the time of graduation, I had already flunked the Marine/Navy eye examination due to the nearsightedness. I was drafted into the Army a few weeks after graduation in July 1943. Initially assigned to the Army Specialized Training Program due to a high score on the Army General Classification test, I spent five idyllic months at Hendrix junior college in Conway, Arkansas after 13 weeks of infantry basic training in Ft. Hood, Texas. When the ASTP program was folded-up in order to provide replacements for infantry divisions, our group at Hendrix College was sent to the 99th Infantry Division at Camp Maxey on the Texas/Oklahoma border near the town of Paris, Texas. A second basic training reduced to 9 weeks ensued followed by unit training and so forth. I wound up as the Browning automatic rifleman in my squad commanded by Staff Sgt. Howell, who was my nemesis and had me assigned to KP on practically every Sunday when we weren't in the field.

If I had not been nearsighted, I would have gone into a Navy or Marine V-12 program and stayed on some campus for the duration, but as it was, the ASTP was slated to join the Infantry well before the war was over, and I have recounted that experience in "The Short Life of the ASTP." I went in as a private and came out as a PFC, and initially felt extreme frustration in not being a noncom or a commissioned officer. As time passed, these cares were no longer of any importance, but having been part of the final defense of Elsenborn Ridge in Belgium against the Germans in the Battle of the Bulge was. I had a Purple Heart, Bronze Star, and most important, a Combat Infantry Badge to show for my service.

Discharge into civilian life was completely disorienting at first. As I drove or walked around the friendly hills of home, I found myself constantly looking for a place to put machine guns or mortars, and I kept a loaded .45 near at hand in my bedroom for a long time. Contact with other veterans made a big difference. My neighbor, Dan Brewster, had served as a Marine platoon leader at Guam and Okinawa, and had been wounded several times. Miles ("Boo") White had served in the 11th Armored Division and he and Ned Goodnow, who was in my company in the 99th Division, shared a crowded suite of rooms with three others at Princeton in the Fall of 1946.

CHAPTER 3
PRINCETON, LAW SCHOOL, ETC.

I started at Princeton in the fall of 1946 as a sophomore since Johns Hopkins had given me credit for one semester for my five months in ASTP at Hendrix College and I had a full semester at Hopkins. In turn, Princeton credited anything that Hopkins did. As already stated, because of the number of returning veterans to campus, Boo White, Ned Goodnow, and I roomed with three others in a small suite designed for three, not six persons. Sleeping was in double-decker bunks. Boo White was a merry companion as a roommate with an unflagging sense of humor and quick wit. He and I felt that we had a special bond as infantry veterans and occasionally walked the darkened streets of Princeton after a session at the Nassau Tavern singing "Waltzing Matilda" and "Lily Marlene." I would never have believed in those days that later he would commit suicide despondent over a failed marriage and mounting debts that effectively eliminated his chances for becoming president of one of the leading banks in Baltimore.

In retrospect, I'm sorry that I started as a sophomore. I should have taken more time in the educational process. My major was history, though I had taken many courses in the scientific path at St. Paul's. It may have been the experience of the war that headed me in the liberal arts direction. Princeton had a great history department faculty: Mommsen in early Medieval, Harbison in Renaissance and Reformation, R.R. Palmer on Revolutionary Europe, and Goldman in Modern Diplomatic history. There were other attractions such as Carlos Baker in Shakespeare and courses in German that I was impelled to take beginning with 10 hours a week of colloquial German followed by German literature and a senior year on Goethe in which all lectures and classes were given in German, essays written in the language and so forth. I was captivated by Goethe, Thomas Mann, and Gerhardt Hauptman.

Princeton used the precept system and your senior paper represented 50% of your final class standing. I graduated magna cum laude because of intense efforts spent in my final year working on a paper about Joseph Chamberlain, Neville's father, and his position in the British Liberal Party. Harriet and I were married at the end of my sophomore year; so my orientation was away from campus social life, though I joined the Ivy Club and played on its intramural hockey team at Baker rink. Because of the housing shortage, we lived in five different locations during the last two years of university life with our firstborn, Hallie, finally buying a house in a development on Harrison Street across from Mac and Ramsay Raymond, who later became very good friends, he being a member of the class of 1940 and an assistant dean. Our social life with them was oriented

24

towards young faculty members, graduate students, and university administrative personnel.

My experience in World War II is recounted in a short memoir, "The Short Life of the ASTP" and it should not be surprising that the experience radicalized me to a certain extent. I considered industrial workers as the equivalent of front line infantrymen and identified with labor and the Democratic Party. In addition, I joined the American Veterans Committee which was the only racially integrated veterans' organization at the time. Its founder, Charles Bolte, had enlisted in the British Army and lost a leg at El Alamein. The organizational slogan was "Citizens first, Veterans second;" meaning that we supported the GI bill, but not bonus marches. AVC absorbed much of my energy and was a great educational experience in itself. One learned how to organize demonstrations, to know Roberts rules of order, and to work with African-American members of the Baltimore community. These activities occurred in Baltimore in 1946 before going to Princeton in September and later during college vacation periods. Though I believe that I would have joined AVC anyhow, one incident that occurred shortly after I got home from overseas propelled me in that direction. I was at Penn Station waiting to get a train to New York and saw a young, black GI in uniform with a 99th Division checkerboard patch on his right shoulder, showing that he had belonged to one of those volunteer platoons of black soldiers who had volunteered from rear echelon jobs in port battalions and trucking companies when the need for infantry replacements was at its greatest at the close of the Battle of the Bulge. I said hello to him and asked what regiment he had been in and so forth, and asked about his present status. He said that he had re-enlisted because he simply could not stand the segregation of civilian life that he encountered coming home. It reminded me of the volunteer platoon that had been assigned to my company after the Bulge, which I had seen in action as we made an assault crossing of the Danube River after my return from various hospitals for repair of wounds incurred in action.

I had joined my first picket line at the AVC convention in Des Moines in the summer of 1946, protesting the management of a bar that refused service to black delegates attending the convention. Black members at home who became good friends were Clark Davis, manager of the Cherry Hill housing project; Walter Fisher on the Morgan college faculty; Bob Lee, a local movie theater owner whose wife Lena became a member of the Maryland House of Delegates; and Dr. Eugene D. Byrd, an orthodontist. Other active members were Bill Boucher, later Executive Director of the Greater Baltimore Committee; Sandy Frank, whose firm made linings for coats; Leonard Rosenberg, future President of Chesapeake Life Insurance Company; Herb

Fedder, an accountant; Bob Hendrickson, who worked for the City Housing Authority; Dick Marshall, both a teacher and insurance agent; and Mal Sherman, who is still active in real estate today. My neighbor and childhood friend, Dan Brewster, the future U.S. Senator, was an early AVC member and shocked the ladies of the Greenspring Valley by having Clark Davis come to a meeting at his family's house. It was said that he was entertaining negroes on a social basis. It was hard to realize how segregated Baltimore was in those days. We successfully integrated the Park Plaza Hotel near Mt. Vernon square by having dinner meetings there as shown in the photograph on page 37.

In addition, there was an important lesson learned when the Communist party tried to infiltrate the organization to convert it to a bonus marching mass organization to support the Realpolitik of the Big Three: Britain, Soviet Russia, and the USA rather than the newly formed United Nations. There were other twists and turns in the party line. The culmination occurred at the national convention in Cleveland in 1948 when a member of the board named Morris Potash was expelled for following the party line. I wound up as a teller of ballots in a locked room. Across the table were three members of the New York Labor party attired in black leather jackets. It was an intense proceeding.

1948 was the year that I first was eligible to vote in a Presidential election. Boo White and I traveled home by train and argued all the way down about our choices. I said that I was for Truman and he was for Norman Thomas. On the return trip to Princeton, Boo confessed that he had finally wound up voting for Dewey as he wanted to be on the winning side.

I have tried to describe my disorientation on returning home from the war in my memoir titled "The Short Life of the ASTP." Nevertheless, I seemed to be pretty well adjusted to university life and newly married status. An early crisis with the Soviet Union in 1948 over the take-over in Czechoslovakia when Jan Masryk was thrown out of a window by Communist agents started me on the road to a deep depression. It appeared we might be going to war with our former ally. The depression became so bad that I found myself talking to the university psychiatrist, who said that I was far from unique as many other veteran students were having similar problems. He started me on "uppers" and "downers" which helped, but made it very difficult to control the medication balance. At exam time during my junior year, I found that I was either writing so slowly and lethargically that I could barely finish the exam, or writing so feverishly that my handwriting became indecipherable. Somehow I managed to get through the term and started working on my senior thesis.

As my time at Princeton drew to a close, I realized that I had to decide what to do for a career other than going to AVC meetings. Writing history and college teaching beckoned, but my adviser made it clear that junior faculty members could not obtain tenure anywhere for many years, and we would have to move from university to university. Being married with one child and another on the way did not set the stage for such a career and I decided on law school as a second choice. In addition, my mother was very ill. My father had died in 1944 and there were family obligations in Baltimore to take care of.

I enrolled in the University of Maryland Law School. At the first lecture in a crowded first floor amphitheater-type room, the professor told us to look at the person to our right and left because by the second year half the class would be gone. We had the grand total of two young women as members of the class, Hugo Hoffman's step-daughter, Arle Ann Perry, and Elsbeth Levy, later Bothe. Arle Ann dropped out after the first year but Elsbeth courageously hung on, eventually becoming a Circuit Court judge in Baltimore. Today the freshman class is more than 50% female.

The case method of studying law was an ice cold dash of water to someone used to reading history and writing essays. In my first year, my grades bumped along at the C level. I did not begin to move up until the second and third year when Constitutional Law and Conflict of Laws caught my fancy, as had Criminal Law and Evidence.

I had joined the Army Reserve shortly after discharge in 1946. Along with others in the same category, we began to worry about our status when the Korean War occurred. A group of us obtained permission to take the Bar examination early in March of our senior year – four hours per day for two consecutive days in the old Richmond Market. I barely passed, but was duly sworn in before the Maryland Court of Appeals and the Federal District Court.

In fact, I missed Korea by about two weeks. At the time that the Korean war started, I still had my old MOS of 746 representing Browning automatic rifleman, though nominally assigned to a paper airborne unit which never got organized, I was still in a pool of unassigned reservists in the Maryland Military District. Towards the end of my second year of law school, an announcement was made that there was a paid status Counter Intelligence Corps unit in Baltimore looking for recruits from the Law School. I immediately put my name in and found myself assigned to the 275th Counter Intelligence Corps detachment which had paid status for weekend drills. Those reservists with infantry MOS designations in the Maryland Military District pool, were being hurriedly called up, sent to Ft. Campbell, Kentucky for six days of weapons refamiliarization and flown directly to Pusan to the beleaguered beach-head, trying to hold off the attacking North Koreans. Comfortably ensconced among the 15 or 20 members of the 275th CIC detachment, I watched the war from afar without any regrets.

Ironically, the non-coms and officers who had had prior experience in counter-intelligence were called up for duty in Korea while those who still had combat arms MOS designations were left behind. I eventually got a commission, went to various reserve schools in intelligence, and retired as a Major. The only "active" duty that I ever saw was posting a situation map in the Baltimore County Civil Defense Headquarters during the 1968 riots.

In spite of the difficulty in adapting to the case method of study, the three years in the Law School were not entirely unpleasant, and I found most of the fellow students to be congenial and well educated. Some of us got together regularly for lunch: Ben Cadwalader of Harford County, Bob Price of Centerville, and Lansdale (Gus) Sasscer of Upper Marlboro. Ben, a slow speaker, had a very dry sense of humor. He had served as an artillery liaison pilot in the 29th Division in World War II and was still active. One day he asked me if I would like to go up with him as he needed to get in some flying hours. We proceeded to Harbor Field and he told me to pick up a parachute, but as we approached the Piper Cub, he told me to take it off as both it and I could not fit through the cockpit door at the same time, not a very consoling thought. Bob Price coasted through law school with canned briefs and got the second highest mark on the Bar examination.

Even in those days, the law school had an excellent faculty. The best teachers were those with idiosyncratic personalities that enhanced rather than detracted from their teaching. For example, Strahorn taught Criminal Law and Evidence. He would draw a chart on the blackboard behind his desk, divided into various slices of a pie representing degrees of theft ranging from embezzlement to grand larceny. He would call on a member of the class to state what part of the chart a certain offense fell in, and would rock back in his chair stabbing his thumb at the unseen chart behind him to illustrate what he was talking about. He would lean over so far backwards in his chair that we would hold our breath waiting for him to fall, but he never did. In Evidence during the second year to illustrate the fallacy of eyewitness testimony, he would suddenly jump up and rush to the window pointing at an animal laboratory across the alley maintained by the University hospital and shout "Do you see the monkey over there?!" Assistant Dean Bridgewater Arnold was outstanding as a teacher of creditor's rights and we filed away his phrase "Put the writ in the mitt" to illustrate when a judgment lien becomes effective at the time of levy. Reno had Real Property I and II and Probate Law. Kenneth Reiblich taught Constitutional Law and was truly eccentric. It was rumored he had driven his teenage son around the bend so far that the young man tried to climb the Washington monument holding on to the lightning rod cable before being apprehended by the police. Another original was "Colonel" Ruge, born and raised in the Florida panhandle near Tallahassee, who taught Contracts and Corporation Law. A Roosevelt-hater, he would tell the class well in advance that on a certain date he was going to give a lecture on The New Deal, which would be optional for all students. Naturally, everyone turned out for the occasion to hear his diatribe. A court decision that he disagreed with was referred to as "bum law." "Whitey" Farinhold was an excellent teacher of Torts, though lacking in the eccentricities already mentioned. Reuben Oppenheimer, later a member of the Court of Appeals, taught Conflict of Laws, a fascinating subject. Larry Jones gave us all the basics in Real Property III. The dullest, though a very important course, i.e. Negotiable Instruments, was taught by the dullest member of the faculty, Fred Invernizzi, but there was nothing he could have done to have enlivened the subject matter.

Practice court was held on Monday evenings and customarily some of us repaired to Murray's Musical Bar, a strip joint, a short half-block from the Law School after the evening session. One time, we decided to take Gus Sasscer to give him a little education as he appeared to have lived a rather sheltered life. He seemed grateful when the rest of us decided it was time to leave. The next day he approached me rather diffidently and asked if I would do him a great favor; namely, to go with him to the bar where he thought he had left a case book. When we walked into the semi-darkness of the bar from the bright sunshine of the early October day, it seemed to be crowded with longshoremen and other local types – no bar girls. Gus cleared his throat a few times and asked the bartender if by any chance someone had found a book that he had left there. That request produced silence as all heads turned towards this person who had gone into the bar with a book in hand. Eventually, Gus got a note from one of the bar girls saying that she had it and would be glad to personally deliver it to him, an offer I do not believe he accepted. Now attending class reunions at the new Law School is like physically passing from one era into another in terms of accommodation and layout.

Another classmate was the younger Tommy D'Alesandro, later mayor of the City. He was not a very apt student and a tutorial team was formed to get him through consisting of the late Frank Gallagher with assistance from Carmen Granese and another resident of Little Italy. They managed to pull him through.

Ben Cadwalader became a highly respected member of the Bar in Bel Air and was an equity master for many years. Bob Price, later joined by his son, established a very successful practice in Centerville. Gus Sasscer eventually became the senior partner in his father's former law firm in Upper Marlboro.

1952 was a tough year to land a job in a law firm. A number of our brighter law school classmates took government jobs, and the rest of us walked the streets for some time. However, I was contacted by Warren Buckler, partner in one of the larger firms now Niles, Barton & Wilmer, to see if I would be interested in an associate position in the firm working with him. He was a specialist in municipal bond issues and had a very liberal reputation. He was also a member of the Baltimore City Council and often embroiled in issues of municipal segregation.

Warren was almost totally blind and I delayed acting on his offer, perhaps because my instinct suggested I would become a glorified "gofer" for him, and not have an opportunity to develop my own practice. He invited me to have lunch at the prestigious Hamilton Street Club which boasted prominent newspaper editors, academics, and lawyers such as William L. Marbury among its members. I was quite awed by the assembly, particularly when I learned that the guest speaker was none other than the famous author, John Dos Passos. I cannot remember what Dos Passos' topic was, but the entire discussion turned towards Alger Hiss, who had been convicted of perjury in 1950. The question on everybody's mind was was he really guilty or not. It seemed that every member of the Hamilton Street Club believed in Hiss's innocence, the speaker being apparently in a minority of one. He said that he had experience with Communists which the members had not, probably referring to what he had seen in Spain during the civil war. I nodded a quiet agreement because of my own brief experience in AVC dealing with CPUSA District 4 Communist party members who kept us up to all hours of the night trying to outlast us in meetings. Ironically, the meeting I remember when the division with the party liners came into the open was at the Friends meeting house on Charles Street across from the Hopkins Homewood campus. Later when the division became acute at the national level, the anti-Communists formed a caucus known as the Independent Progressive Caucus. The other side called themselves the Unity Caucus. It was expected that there would be a purge of a member of the National Board and to prepare for it, we had an intense caucus meeting in Washington, organized by Gus Tyler, who had been a labor organizer for the Dubinsky Garment Workers Union and reputedly at one time a Trotskyite. That all had occurred in 1948. In 1952, I definitely was not interested in municipal bond issue legal work and I thanked Warren Buckler and continued my job search.

American Veterans Committee - Baltimore Chapter No. 1

(From left to right) <u>Sitting</u>: Andy Rice, Harriet Iglehart, Dick Marshall, Francis Iglehart, Herb Fedder, Edna Rosenberg / <u>Standing</u>: Robert Nathan (?), unidentified, Bob Lee, Dan Brewster, unidentified, unidentified (middle of window), Emily Marshall (directly in front), Elaine Davis, Leonard Rosenberg, Walter Fisher, unidentified (below wall lamp), Clarke Davis, unidentified, George Arrowsmith, Bob Hendrickson, unidentified

CHAPTER 4
FRANCE, ROUZER & HARRIS

The summer of 1952 had not been an easy time to obtain a job in a law office, and I did not obtain a position until August as a very junior associate in the firm of France, Rouzer & Harris. Two partners, William Lentz and Charles Page, had left to form their own firm. Another partner, Kenneth C. Proctor, had returned from the war and opened his own practice in Towson. He knew Harriet's father and made the telephone call that got me the job. Jacob France was chairman of the Maryland Republican Party as well as chairman of the board at Midcontinent Petroleum and The Equitable Trust Company. E. McClure Rouzer specialized in estate work and taxation. Charles Harris was office manager and People's Counsel to the Public Service Commission.

I was assigned a tiny office, later used as a coffee room, at the magnificent salary of $55 per week and half of any fees that I brought in to the office. Hired at the same time was Walter Tabler, a year ahead of me at law school who had been doing defense work for Liberty Mutual Insurance Company in the workmens' compensation field. He started at a salary of $65 per week plus half of his fees. Walter was aggressive in developing a workmens' compensation practice to such an extent that Mr. Harris told him that he should spend more time on firm matters rather than his own cases. Depending upon his salary and fees with a growing family, Walter was soon getting compensation cases from Joe Neal at the Steelworkers Union, and developed a successful practice of his own.

My own practice, such as it was, was more diverse. During the summer of my second year in law school, I worked as an unpaid volunteer at the Legal Aid Bureau under the then director, Gerald Monsman. Working with hapless, destitute clients in an unair-conditioned office during a Baltimore summer was an ordeal. It was Mr. Monsman's philosophy to take any case regardless of its merits. I was assigned to work with the late Deems Barnard in landlord/tenant matters, and we suffered some stinging rebukes from members of the bench for presenting our fanciful theories to help tenants trying to make ends meet.

If an applicant for Legal Aid was over the income limit for assistance, he or she was referred out to a panel of lawyers who had worked for the organization. I was one and received some interesting referrals. One of the first involved a black, Army major who had served in Korea, named Wejay Bundara. He needed advice concerning his interest in leasing a trucking garage up near Pennsylvania Avenue in Baltimore City. It turned out that the owner of the garage was the famed numbers king, "Little Willie" Adams, whom I met at the site to discuss terms. After looking over the facility, we repaired to his office where Mr. Adams speculated as to which of his many attorneys he would refer my draft of the lease to for review. Apparently he had 7 or 8 who handled different aspects of his business empire in addition to personal criminal defense work. Many years later during a period of extreme drought in the summer of 1965, I was helping unload a shipment of hay from the Finger Lakes region of New York State at our farm. The truck driver said we had a nice place, but the most beautiful farm of any that he had seen in Maryland was on the shores of the Susquehanna River owned by a black gentleman named Willie Adams. I said that I had met Mr. Adams once before.

Jacob France was an eminence rarely seen; in my case, I believe only once in two years. Mr. Rouzer was short, balding, and a veteran of The Lost Battalion in World War I. He had a kindly eye and manner and I remember him fondly. Charles Harris, later a Circuit Court judge, was a very handsome man who had worked as a male model and his interest in the ladies must have made life difficult for his wife.

The firm was run to a very significant extent by Mr. France's secretary of many, many years, Miss Julia Knoerr, who cut the payroll checks and was the only notary public in the office. She ruled the secretarial pool with an iron hand and banished mini-skirts from the office. We were located in the Equitable Building across the street from the bank. Coming in after a short Christmas break when all the windows had been closed and the steam heat still going, we found our only decoration – a small, live tree denuded of its ornaments and needles in a state of total collapse. I told Walter Tabler that that was a good indication of the spirit of the office.

One time, Walter had a black client, Clarence DeWitt, who had fractured his skull in a fall from a gangplank while pushing a wheelbarrow to a building foundation. Johns Hopkins affixed a plaster turban on his head. Because of his tendency to drink up his workmen's compensation benefits, Walter doled out the money to him carefully. Once a week, he waited in the outer office with a battered, tweed cap perched on his head above the turban. Miss Julia got quite exercised by the appearance of this apparition, which she said was disturbing to the elderly ladies who were coming to see Mr. Rouzer for review of their wills and estate plans, and Clarence was banished to an empty office where Herb Hubbard had been ensconced before taking a position in the U.S. Attorney's office. Mr. Rouzer was quite startled one day to walk into Herb's office looking for a tax service to be confronted by Clarence in his turban.

It was a real learning experience as Walter and I were thrust into handling matters that we were not trained for or experienced in, such as writing tax memos for Mr. Rouzer and even representing the beneficiary of a family trust who was trying to change its terms. One of my darker moments in the early practice of law was having to appear before Judge Emory Niles on law motion day and arguing an issue about which I was totally unprepared, being asked by Judge Niles why a certain rule didn't apply about which I was totally ignorant.

My career at France, Rouzer & Harris was pretty effectively shortened by a case of polio in late November of 1954 when I spent time in the polio ward at City Hospital, then Children's, and finally discharged to live in the family house at Ivy Hill where our mother had a first floor bedroom, she no longer living there having rented an apartment in the City. After about three months of being bedridden, I was on crutches for another 6 to 8 months and then on a cane, and began driving with my first hydramatic shift in an Oldsmobile because of the condition of my left leg. I began spending some time in a small office I had rented in Towson and started working on my first big case – a blasting case!

What follows is a sample of the extremely varied types of cases that I was involved in, typical of a general practice. As the reader will see, I won some, lost some, and had a draw in others.

CHAPTER 5
SCHOOL DESEGREGATION

In the summer of 1954, an unexpected confluence of my prior membership and work in AVC coupled with having a new law degree compelled me to do something that I never would have done as a mere private citizen. I am referring to the Supreme Court decision in <u>Brown v. Board of Education</u> and the Baltimore Board of Education vote to desegregate all schools in the City the following Fall as a result, though Baltimore could hardly be considered in the vanguard of desegregation. There were days of violent demonstrations and assaults on blacks in the vicinity of many schools. The situation at Southern High School was among the worst. Clark Davis said that he was more afraid going through that area than during his time in New Guinea in the war.

Though the AVC chapter in Baltimore was now mostly a paper organization, I felt impelled to do something and called Dick Marshall, who was chapter chairman, suggesting that we talk to the City police commissioner, Col. Beverly Ober, formerly of the Maryland National Guard. The appointment was made for the Elkridge Club at 5 pm on a Saturday afternoon when the disturbances were assumed to have subsided. On the way to the Elkridge Club on Charles Street, something told me to stop and check the Maryland Code which I did at the office I was leasing on Washington Avenue in

Towson. Rather than looking at Article 27, setting forth the Maryland Criminal Code, I went to Article 77 on Public Education and found there a section that made it a misdemeanor to "disturb" public schools while in session.

When Dick Marshall and I met with Col. Ober over mint juleps at the club, I told him of the section and suggested that he enforce it. Second-hand information after the event was to the effect that Col. Ober called the member of the Maryland Attorney General staff with responsibility for schools and received a noncommittal answer, following which he contacted Steve Sachs' father who had gotten him a cheaper price for police uniforms in his business. Mr. Sachs apparently told Col. Ober that the two ex-GIs seemed to be on the right track and the Colonel made his decision, going on the air before the opening of schools on Monday citing Article 77 and threatening to arrest anyone demonstrating in front of schools. This action cooled things off considerably, though a rabblerouser named Bryant Bowles, who claimed the title as head of the National Association for the Advancement of White People, had come to Baltimore over the weekend and organized a mass rally at Ritchie Raceway in Anne Arundel County. It was a powerful lession in the efficacy of the law.

CHAPTER 6
THE HORSE WORLD

After graduating from Princeton in 1949, Harriet and I purchased from Oldfields School a cottage on the top of the hill behind Hillside, her parents' house, in Glencoe. A neighbor not too far away on Irish Avenue was Colonel Jacob Pearce, USMC (Ret.). When the Korean War broke out the following year, Col. Pearce was contacted by General Lemuel Shepperd, an old Marine Corps buddy, to see if he could find a home for the General's horse, Circumstance, a 10 year old chestnut gelding that had been a whip horse at Potomac Hunt Club before General Shepperd acquired him. The asking price was only $350, but the proposed buyer had to pass inspection first. General Shepperd was to become Fleet Marine Commander in the Korean Theater and he had to find a home for his horse.

The try-out of the horse and the inspection of the buyer occurred in a stockade-like ring at Quantico where I was asked to mount and proceed to jump various obstacles which the horse negotiated very skillfully. The deal was closed and Circumstance, later nicknamed by us as the "General," arrived a few days later by horse trailer attended by three Marine Corps enlisted men. There ensued several years of pleasant foxhunting experiences with him until I got the racing bug and started entering him in so-called heavyweight events in the

Unionville area, the Elkridge-Harford race at Atlanta Hall Farm, and eventually the Western Run Plate, which was then the second race on the day of the Maryland Grand National over the same course, a fairly formidable one.

We soon found out that General had great jumping ability but absolutely no speed at all, which didn't bother me. The main problem was in order to make the weight of 185 pounds, I had to carry more than 20 pounds of lead, making an awkward saddle arrangement. Fellow competitors were Dan Brewster, Colonel Rossell, Peter Winants, Jay Secor, Jack Devereux, and others. A photograph in the old living room shows Peter Winants, Jay Secor, and me jumping the first fence in one of the Unionville races. Jay was on a very rank steed named "Bomber," who we tried to stay away from. When the day of the Maryland Grand National arrived in 1953, I felt that I was as ready as I could be.

Having stabled my horse with the Smithwicks at the Elkridge-Harford Hunt Club, I followed their advice on vitamins and galloped with them. Mikey and Paddy Smithwick were amused at General's high chopping gait which tended to diminish his speed. They nicknamed him "Chopper." Mikey was going to ride some horse in the Western Run Plate and said that he would check me out in the paddock and make sure all of my gear was in place, the girth properly cinched, and so forth.

One of the entries was a horse owned by Paul Mellon named White Coat and it promised to be a very fast race, much faster than General and I were prepared for, as I soon found out shortly after the flag was dropped. As we hurtled along, I soon had the feeling "What in the h*** was I doing?" Coming into the fourth fence where the main crowd was normally located, Mikey turned in his saddle four strides from the fence, a four foot post and rail affair, and shouted "Follow me!" The lead was a good one and we negotiated the course dead last to light applause.

The next year, there were no White Coats in the race and the main competition was Jack Devereux and Dan Brewster. We finished third out of five with two "fallers." My bout with polio in late November of that year effectively ended my racing career for quite a while.

General at Quantico

CHAPTER 7
FIRST JURY TRIAL

While I was in the hospital in November, 1954, the Bethlehem Steel Company entered into a contract with C. J. Langenfelder & Sons to install a large water line from the Baltimore sewage disposal plant down along the North Point Road to the mill. At a place called Bread & Cheese Creek, Langenfelder was using a technique called a dynamite fill, placing explosives in the swampy area and dropping pipe in immediately after the explosions displaced the muck. An elderly, retired foundry owner from east Baltimore named William Kneis complained that the explosions were causing the ground to shake, cracking hundreds of panes of glass in his greenhouses where he was raising azaleas for the wholesale market. He wanted to sue, and, for some reason, had tried to contact me, perhaps as part of the Legal Aid Bureau referral system. I thought the case would be an easy one since we had been taught in law school about the English case of Fletcher v. Rylands holding that a coal mine owner could sue an adjacent neighbor under the theory of absolute liability as a result of water seeping into the mine from the adjacent property - a type of trespass, proof of negligence not being required. The insurance carrier for the defendants was Maryland Casualty represented by the late Michael Paul Smith soon to become a member of the bench for the Circuit Court of

Baltimore County. He said he thought my theory was sound and that he would recommend a reasonable settlement. Unfortunately, shortly thereafter, he was elevated to the bench and defense of the case was assigned to a young, very brash associate, named W. Lee Harrison, who was instructed to make it a test case with no thought of settlement.

I made a mistake in drafting the suit by not limiting the theory to a single count of absolute liability under Fletcher v. Rylands, having a second count in negligence. The case was tried before Judge Lester L. Barrett and a jury for more than three weeks. Over my objection, Judge Barrett permitted the defendants to use the testimony of Frank Cicone, a Maryland Casualty insurance adjuster and years later a Circuit Court judge, to testify to readings on a seismograph placed in the vicinity of the Kneis property. At the end of testimony, Judge Barrett instructed the jury on the law of nuisance rather than negligence or absolute liability. I had engaged as an expert witness the head of the Geology Department at Johns Hopkins University, Professor Cloos, who testified that the dynamite fill process was similar to situations he had seen on the Texas Gulf coast where oil was being explored for, the blasting causing the super-saturated soil to shake like jello in a bowl. Dr. Cloos was an excellent geologist but a very poor courtroom witness, often getting flustered in cross-examination and having a thick, German

50

accent. In an audacious move, Lee Harrison signed up Dr. Cloos' number 2 man in the department as a witness against him claiming that his theory was wrong and that soil type in the area would have a dampening effect on the blasting vibrations. The number 2 man had no accent and was a glib, easily understandable witness. The jury was out for 7 hours and finally came back with a defendant's verdict. A hard lesson for my first jury case!

I was physically and emotionally drained, still recovering from the effects of polio. It was small consolation that 6 other cases that I had against Langenfelder and Bethlehem Steel for property owners who had had damage to their houses were quickly settled by the insurance carrier to avoid another marathon ordeal in the Circuit Court.

CHAPTER 8
DEFECTIVE DELINQUENTS

While in the City Hospital polio ward, I had a practical nurse on night duty whose maiden name was Millsap from the South Carolina hill country. I was going through often excruciating pain and could not sleep at all until she, Jacqueline ("Jackie"), would bring me several cups of strong, black coffee around midnight which for some strange reason did the trick and sent me off to slumberland. After discharge from City Hospital and then Children's Hospital, I slowly regained my ability to walk with the help of the eminent physical therapist, H. O. Kendall, and began practicing law again starting with a very rough beginning in the blasting case. In those days, there was no Public Defender's office and local members of the bar were routinely appointed in criminal cases where the defendant was lacking in funds. In addition to criminal cases, I was appointed to represent various inmates of Patuxent Institute where those who were deemed qualified as defective delinquents under a new statute were housed. Patuxent Institute was the brainchild of a University of Maryland Law School professor, Kenneth Reiblich, who taught Constitutional Law. He held an ardent belief that criminals could be rehabilitated through group therapy and psychiatric analysis. A convicted criminal could be referred by a sentencing judge to Patuxent for evaluation, and if found to fit the statute, could be held for any length of time while being rehabilitated. The period of incarceration could be longer or shorter than the original sentence. I was appointed to represent several inmates whose cases were tried before juries and all of whom were sent back to Patuxent.

Then my old night nurse, Jackie, called me to ask if I would represent her brother, Harold, who was in Patuxent and who wanted out. In addition to Harold, she had an older brother named Gilbert, who had served as an infantryman in Korea and for a time was on the FBI Most Wanted List for armed robbery. Harold was only a petty thief and his referral to Patuxent had resulted from breaking into a warehouse with several confederates to pilfer materials stored there. Twice I tried Harold's case before juries in Towson and each time wound up with a hung jury. In each case, my skill in cross-examination of staff members at Patuxent improved as I learned the psychiatric lingo and the meaning of the term "sociopath." In addition to being a sociopath, the staff agreed that Harold was also part of a subculture to which his actions were not inappropriate. In fact, as children he and Gilbert had for a time lived and slept in a boxcar parked on a rail siding near the penitentiary. Their mother was working on "The Block." Finally, on the third try I was successful and the new jury sprung Harold Millsap to joy of his sister. Less than two months later, he was shot dead in an attempt to hold up a pharmacy for drugs, which made me feel somewhat better about the other cases I had lost. Harold had lived and died in accordance with the tenets of his subculture.

CHAPTER 9
THE VAN HORN CASE

Though this is supposed to be a personal account of dealing with the vagaries of the law, I have to mention the Van Horn case which gripped the local legal community and held me spellbound for several days in the old Circuit Courtroom in Towson listening to the testimony. What follows was gleaned from newspaper clippings at the time.

Early on June 3, 1957, the crew of a cruising police car stopped to check on a parked stationwagon on an uncompleted section of I-83 near Joppa Road which had a man seated behind the steering wheel. The driver was Robert J. Van Horn, a 52 year old lumber company executive and a prominent member of the Maryland and Baltimore Country Clubs. In one hand he held a .32 caliber automatic and in the other a glass of whiskey. A stand-off ensued as Van Horn threatened to shoot himself. Other police arrived including Inspector Ellison Ensor and Detective Capt. Elmer F. Adams. Adams reached through a stationwagon window and seized Van Horn's hand which held the loaded automatic. Thirty feet down an embankment along side the roadbed, police found the severely beaten body of Mrs. Bernice Ward Van Horn, age 53. Mr. and Mrs. Van Horn had been married approximately two years. She had been the widow of Joseph J. Flynn, President of the Monumental Brick and Supply Company, who had been active in Democratic party politics because of his close friendship with former Senator Herbert R. O'Connor. The subsequent autopsy report of the Assistant Medical Examiner indicated that Mrs. Van Horn's injuries were not compatible with those usually associated with a fist beating. All of her ribs were broken in addition to head lacerations. Van Horn had left an extensive written statement in a sealed envelope marked for Baltimore County Police in his office. The statement admitted the killing and expressed deep remorse. Subsequent investigation of the crime established that the murder had occurred at the parties' estate on Falls Road about a mile north of John Brown's store. There were some indications that the stationwagon had been used to inflict Mrs. Van Horn's fatal injuries, as a result of blood stains found on the grass there and hanks of hair found clinging to a tree.

Van Horn was found sitting in the stationwagon on early Sunday morning. The previous Saturday night, the couple attended a party in the vicinity of Winchester, Virginia and consumed an unspecified amount of alcoholic beverages and had no dinner. Apparently there had been a long-running difference of opinion between husband and wife as to whether to move to the country estate, and after driving there the fatal argument occurred.

The case was prosecuted by State's Attorney Frank H. Newell III, and his assistant, Douglas G. Bottom. Defense counsel were

State Senator John Grason Turnbull, Hilary Gans, and William G. Boyce, who entered a plea of not guilty by reason of insanity. Van Horn underwent psychiatric examination three times at Johns Hopkins Hospital, and tests at University Hospital under order from Judge Lester L. Barrett at the request of the State's Attorney. From August 23 to September 21, he was confined to Spring Grove Hospital where he was examined by doctors designated by the State Department of Mental Hygiene. It is this writer's recollection that defense counsel never applied for bail for their client, who remained either in the Baltimore County jail or in the various medical institutions where he underwent psychiatric examinations until the time of trial. Other than the trial, the last time that this writer saw Mr. Van Horn was in the County jail, sitting disconsolately on a bunk in his cell when the author went to see another client, and is embarrassed to remember blurting out "Mr. Van Horn, the last time I saw you was when you were in the winner's circle at Delaware Park," a reference to his ownership of a champion hurdle horse named Ring of Roses trained by D. Michael Smithwick and ridden by A.P. "Paddy" Smithwick.

The case finally went to trial on October 23, 1957 before Judges Barrett, Michael Paul Smith, and Chief Judge John B. Gontrum. What ensued was a battle of psychiatrists, including Dr. David Abramson, Dr. Manuel Hammer, Dr. Israel S. Wexler, all of New York, and Dr. Earl Walker, neurosurgeon at Johns Hopkins. Four notes written by Van Horn were read into evidence in which he asked forgiveness, lamenting the death of his wife, who he said had suddenly struck him with a handbag as they walked down the steps of the house on the country estate after a brief argument. His testimony was to the same effect. He said that he saw red and struck out at her, but could not remember anything at all until he came to after she was dead. There was lay testimony of several epileptic-type seizures that he had had as far back as a football game in prep school many years before. Among the defense character witnesses were Edward Dukehart, President of the Real Estate Board of Baltimore; Frederick L. Wehr, Executive Vice President of the Monumental Life Insurance Company; Charles F. Reese, Vice President of the First National Bank, who had been a fraternity brother at Johns Hopkins; James Piper, Jr., real estate broker; Albert Ward, Secretary of the State Tax Commission; H. Ridgely Warfield, Director of the Johns Hopkins University Institute for Cooperative Research; Chase Ridgely, insurance and real estate broker; and Walter C. Pinkard, Sr., all of whom testified to Van Horn's mild temperament and avoidance of arguments. One defense expert gave the opinion that he had entered into "an epileptic fugue" at the time of the killing. The term puzzled some spectators, who thought that the word "fugue" was solely a musical term.

To the surprise of many, the three judge panel found the Defendant sane beyond a reasonable doubt at the time of the commission of the homicide under the

McNaughton rule. They stated that they had a reasonable doubt as to guilt of first or second degree murder, but were of the unanimous opinion that Van Horn was guilty of manslaughter. He was sentenced to ten years in the State penitentiary and was paroled in January 1961.

A sad epilogue to the Van Horn story followed his 1969 marriage to another widow, Evelyn Monte, with whom he lived in a retirement condominium in Connecticut. On June 2, 1987, the 83 year old former Baltimore lumber executive took a shotgun and killed his second wife and then turned the weapon on himself. When the neighbors there described the impression they had of Robert Van Horn, the words took on a strangely familiar ring. He was "always very quiet, always a gentleman" one neighbor said. "Very polite" said another. These were the same words used by his character witnesses in the 1957 Baltimore County murder trial.

CHAPTER 10
AN EXPERT WITNESS

One day, not long after the Van Horn case had ended, I received a telephone call from my nephew, Jack Howard, who was quite perturbed. He said that Baltimore Gas & Electric (BG&E) was tearing up the roadway of Greenspring Avenue north of Valley Road for a major natural gas distribution line. Jack said that he understood that all of the deeds within the family called to the center line of Greenspring Avenue, and, therefore, BG&E was trespassing on our property without permission. It was a situation that required immediate action, but the problem was what to do. In fact, Greenspring Avenue was an ancient roadway established by vehicular use without condemnation or dedication of the right-of-way. Reputedly, it had been an Indian trail to a camping ground which was then a pasture field originally owned by my family at the southeast corner of Greenspring Avenue and Valley Roads. One of the Ivy Hill tenant houses had been a log cabin. I explained to Jack that stopping the project by obtaining an injunction would be too expensive as we might have to post a bond worth millions of dollars, but I said that I would try to think of something. Through the grapevine, I had heard that a civil engineer, Jerome B. Wolff, later to become a prominent friend of Ted Agnew's, might be able to provide expert witness testimony to underpin the claim for monetary damages.

I contacted Jerry Wolff, who sounded interested in the problem, and said that he would be glad to get to work on it. His approach was to look up and obtain copies of hundreds of pages of testimony in a U.S. Senate hearing on the relative safety of natural gas pipelines from which he extrapolated the frequency with which serious explosions could be expected to occur on these lines over a 100 year time span. Since we were at year zero, it meant that the frequency factor was relatively small, but real nevertheless.

Another factor that might limit the damage was that this stretch of Greenspring Avenue proceeded through a very steep cut because of the extreme grade going north. Presumably, the banks of the cut would act as some barrier against damage from any explosion. Regardless of this, I filed suit and engaged a well known, local real estate appraiser, Hugh Gelston, to give us a damage figure for depreciation in value of the houses that our family owned along the roadway. I was surprised at the amount that Gelston came up with, and decided to contact neighbors further down the line with properties on Greenspring Avenue, such as Bob and Ryda Levy, to see if they wanted to join in the litigation, but their attorneys all thought it was a waste of time.

The late Jim Cook, senior partner of a well known Towson firm, entered his appearance for BG&E, and we prepared to do battle with depositions leading up to a trial date. Our ploy worked, for the case was

61

settled for around $10,000, all due to the "expertise" of Jerry Wolff. It seemed that he could act as an expert in practically any kind of situation as I found out several years later when I sued a large housing developer in Harford County, who was creating a massive erosion of topsoil without adequate safeguards on property of several clients that I represented. Jerry Wolff's new capacity was as an expert on soils. The filing of suit in that case produced the desired result in the form of protective barriers which greatly alleviated the situation, but the monetary damage award from Judge Higginbothom in Bel Air was only sufficient to cover the cost of Wolff's fees.

CHAPTER 11
JUDGES

In 1952, when I was admitted to the Bar, there were exactly two Circuit Court judges in Baltimore County, Howard Murray and John Gontrum. The enormous explosion in County population is illustrated by the fact that today we have 16 judges on the Circuit bench in Towson. Selection was on a very unstructured, informal basis in which politics was quite paramount, the backing of key State Senators being the critical factor in appointment. The days of the two-judge bench were long gone before Marvin Mandel created the Judicial Appointment Commissions for various circuits in the State by Executive Order. I served on the first Commission for the Third Circuit consisting of Baltimore and Harford Counties from 1974 until 1982 by election among lawyers practicing in Baltimore County.

One day, I received a telephone call from Dick Reid of the firm Royston, Mueller, McLean & Reid. He said that two politicos in the eastern part of the County were running for a position on the local Commission and it was feared that the whole purpose of the Commission would be destroyed if they won. Would I help out by running too? I said yes and the result was a convincing victory over the politicos who were candidates.

Jack Raine was not appointed but elected as a popular State's Attorney. Initially, Baltimore County did quite well with the quality of appointments made under the old system. Prior to 1959, Lester L. Barrett and then Albert Menchine were appointed. In 1959, James Lindsay, a former State senator and George Berry, Deputy County Solicitor, were appointed. In 1964, Walter Mitchell Jenifer was appointed and the following year Kenneth C. Proctor, both luminaries on the bench. However, a problem had arisen with George Berry within a matter of a few weeks after his appointment. He was considered a good lawyer but apparently found it difficult to face the responsibility of being a judge. In fact, on the day he was sworn in his right hand was shaking so badly he could barely keep it in the air. Often he was seen in the Bar Library, an unusual place for a judge to be, but soon he was calling in sick and weeks stretched into months with no appearance on the bench. There may have also been an alcohol problem, but the basic disability was fear of facing the responsibilities of office.

One Christmas Eve when there were several inches of snow on the ground, I went to my office on Courtland Avenue and was chagrined to see a lady client coming up the walkway with an urgent look on her face before I had time to escape out the back door. She had been served with an Ex Parte Order of Judge Berry's drastically altering the custody and visiting rights with her children and ex-husband with no petition and no hearing.

Obviously something had to be done quickly because the Clerk's office would be closing at 12 noon. I was able to get a secretary to come in to type another Order canceling the first one. I decided that "what was sauce for the goose was sauce for the gander." The next problem was to get Judge Berry's signature on the new Order rescinding the first one. I knew where he lived in Lutherville and drove out there parking the car near his house, observing milk bottles that had been delivered and stuck in the snow, not retrieved by anyone in the Berry household.

Mrs. Berry welcomed me in and said that George would be so glad to see me as he liked having visitors from Towson. She called him and the judge descended in his bathrobe looking somewhat the worse for wear, but we had a pleasant chat about local politics until he finally asked me if there was anything he could do for me. I explained to him about the Ex Parte Order and why it needed to be rescinded since there had been no hearing of any kind and he gladly signed the new Order, which I rushed back to the Clerk's office to get stamped in. I cannot remember what I did about service on the other side, but what we had accomplished was effective temporarily.

The result of the Berry problem was that the powers that be got together and had a special retirement and pension bill introduced in the legislature applying only to George Berry, which was passed and effective in getting him to retire early. The experience was sufficient basis for the creation of the Judicial Disabilities Commission several years later.

Another former Deputy County Solicitor who had unusual characteristics as a member of the bench was Walter Haile, first appointed in 1966. Judge Haile had a slow, ponderous way of transacting business even if it meant reading a case opinion or rule for many minutes at a time while litigants and attorneys waited for his thought process to run its full cycle. Even on the street walking from his home in west Towson, his stride was careful and deliberate. Once the author of this treatise had a case before him for a client who had been rear-ended by a dump truck driven by an employee of the Perdue chicken empire. When the trial date arrived, the truck driver could not be located and we had to start the case with no individual defendant, suggesting there might be no insurance coverage at all. Somehow the insurance company found him in another line of employment driving freight between Baltimore and New York and brought him into court for the second day of trial after he had been on a long trucking run. When the time came for Judge Haile to give the jury instructions on the law of negligence and so forth, he began reading in his slow, monotonous way; whereupon the truck driver fell almost instantly asleep and began snoring to the amusement of the jury. Several times defense counsel and I rose to our feet to try to get the judge's attention so that something could be done about the snorer. Judge Haile seemed oblivious to what was going on in his courtroom in spite of the jury's laughter until we finally made a large noise, clearing our respective throats. Judge Haile looked somewhat startled, but annoyed at being interrupted, and continued with his instructions while the defendant was kept awake by his counsel. Often during recess time in the trial of a case, Judge Haile would remain on the bench alone reviewing his notes and reading. At least no one complained about his not showing up for duty as a trial judge.

CHAPTER 12
DIVORCE

Like most lawyers in general practice, I had a fair number of divorce and child custody matters as long as my stamina held out, but I finally found my excuse to depart the field when a woman client I represented committed suicide. She was married to an asphalt company executive, was childless, and he had a mistress on the side. Trying the case before then judge Paul Dorf producing evidence of the husband's earning capacity, fringe benefits, etc., I was able to obtain for her a very generous alimony award at the end of two days of trial. However, this was not sufficient solace for when the time came to leave the house in Severna Park as a result of the partition sale following the divorce, everything folded in on her, and I learned upon returning from a sailing trip that she had taken her life.

Preceding that was a more successful experience in representing Isadore A., whose father was a principal stockholder and officer of a large ice cream company. Isadore had no talent for business, but his social conscience steered him in the direction of becoming a welfare case worker. His wife, Natalie, was an avaricious type who expected him to do better things, and her constant prodding forced him into becoming a slum lord as well, faced with myriad citations for housing code violations. He eventually tried suicide and Natalie on the way to the hospital was reported to have looked at her wedding ring and expressed concern as to whether it was glass - a telling remark picked up on by Judge McWilliams of the Court of Appeals in a later stage of the legal proceedings.

The divorce case was tried before Judge Shirley Jones then on the Circuit Court for Baltimore City before she became a federal District judge. She awarded Natalie an amount of alimony that exceeded Isadore's net earnings by 25%, presumably on the theory that he would be bailed out by his parents. I was pretty sure that I could obtain a reversal, and we went on up to the Court of Appeals before the Court of Special Appeals became the intermediate court with jurisdiction over all such type of cases. Hall Hammond was Chief Judge and seated next to Judge McWilliams, who later wrote the opinion. Natalie appeared with her younger sister attired in a mini-skirt that had small tassels on the bottom fringe. I can still remember Judge McWilliams nudging Judge Hammond in the side and looking over in the direction of Natalie and her sister. We won on the appeal and the case was remanded for a drastic reduction in alimony to an amount more compatible with Isadore's actual net. I still think a factor in winning the appeal was the mini-skirt.

In the course of all the litigation, Natalie had retained a total of 7 different attorneys whose advice she had repeatedly refused to accept. On remand from the Court of Appeals, she retained a new attorney, an elderly lawyer with offices at 11 E. Lexington Street, the location of my father's old, real estate office. After months of wrangling, he reported to me that he finally had an agreement which we should put on the record before a Judge of the Supreme Bench. On my way to the City Courthouse, I saw an ambulance in front of 11 E. Lexington Street and a stretcher-borne figure being carried out. It was Natalie's attorney, who had had a fatal heart attack after she had again refused to stay with the settlement she had authorized him to propose. Settlement finally occurred but it was a long time in coming and hardly worth a premature death.

CHAPTER 13
AGENCY LAW

A case that I tried in the late 1950s in Towson illustrated the importance of our course in agency law at the Law School. Defendant Jones was an employee of the American Totalisator Company based in East Towson that manufactured and maintained the parimutual ticket machines for racetracks around the country including Pimlico and Laurel. Under his union contract during the month of January when the tracks were closed locally, he was entitled to a mileage allowance for driving to the main company plant to work. This fact alone created an issue of fact as to whether he was an agent of the company for all intents and purposes while he was in transit, either to the racetracks or to the company headquarters.

One morning in January after a light but wet snow, Jones was driving eastbound to the plant on Stevenson Lane in his Plymouth stationwagon with fellow employees as passengers. While crossing York Road and beginning to descend a long hill on Stevenson Lane seeing how other vehicles were skidding on the wet surface, he quickly threw his hydramatic shift from drive into low, causing the wheels to lock up and the car to go completely out of control, hitting the curb and pinning a pedestrian waiting for a bus umbrella in hand. The pedestrian, Dick, suffered permanent injuries to both legs due to the severely comminuted fractures of

71

them. Ironically, Dick was an editor of the Williams and Wilkens medical publishing company in Baltimore, and it was easy to understand his injuries from the charts contained in one of their recent publications.

Jones' policy limits were $25,000 and defense counsel seemed to be sure that they could eliminate his employer, Totalisator, from the case as a co-defendant. Their counsel, a leading senior partner in a City firm, made the bold statement to the jury in opening that the defense would show that Jones had exercised all reasonable care by shifting from drive into low, causing the car to skid uncontrollably, an unavoidable situation. This rash statement was refuted by the wording of the owner's manual obtained from a local dealer that contained a bold letter warning not to shift from drive into a lower gear on a wet or slippery surface.

When the copy of the owner's manual was produced at trial, however, there were various objections and the defense asked for a recess to discuss possible settlement. We had prepared and submitted to the trial judge a comprehensive statement of case law to the effect that subsidizing an employee's travel cost, regardless of his or her destination, could subject the employer to liability on an agency theory. The trial judge agreed that this made the company's liability a jury question and fairly promptly thereafter the case was settled for almost double Jones' policy limits. I felt rather heady after the trial was over, and repaired to the Penn Hotel for a victory libation and the compliments of the various courthouse hangers-on. I often wondered if the company rewrote their union contract as a result.

CHAPTER 14
OTHER ACTIVITIES

In 1950 I was still in law school, but actively involved in a Congressional primary election campaign with Dick Marshall, a teacher at Gilman School, working for Bill Boucher, later Executive Director of the Greater Baltimore Committee. Boucher had graduated from law school but had not passed the Bar. His main backing was from UAW Local 738, the Glenn L. Martin Local in Essex. After a lot of hard work and soul-searching, Dick and I concluded that he was allowing people to assume he was a lawyer and we resigned from the campaign. As expected he was defeated.

In 1952 when I first began working for France, Rouzer & Harris, I became active in another political campaign. Adlai Stevenson was running for President against Dwight Eisenhower and I teamed up again with Dick Marshall, who had been a year ahead of me at Gilman, to work in the Stevenson campaign. The volunteers for Stevenson were spread pretty thin and as we approached the election, Dick and I found that there were many precincts in Baltimore City where the regular Democratic organization was making no effort at all to promote the Presidential candidate. We filled the void with a small organization enlisting young people our own age, particularly attractive women where we could find them. We found that a dozen precincts were ours to do with as we saw fit.

The local Stevenson organization took a somewhat "holier than thou" attitude and refused to endorse or work for local Democratic candidates, but we felt the opposite and put the Congressional candidate, Sam Friedel, on our sample ballots. We worked hard to get the vote out in the black areas around Greenmount Cemetery. Adlai Stevenson was clobbered pretty hard in the election, but Friedel won his Congressional seat by a very narrow margin, later attributing his win to our modest efforts.

In 1958 I embarked on a foolish endeavor running for State's Attorney on a ticket formed by a local attorney, J. Elmer Weisheit. The candidates at the top of the ticket were Joseph Martin, who owned and operated a gear grinding plant on Pulaski Highway, running for County Executive, and J. Elmer Weisheit running for State Senate with me running for the prosecuting attorney's post held in the County held by one Frank Newell. We were opposing two halves of an entrenched Democratic political machine headed on the one hand by Michael J. Birmingham and Christian H. Kahl. The main image I have of the campaign are three enlarged photographs of Martin, Weisheit, and yours truly plastered on the front of the number 8 buses. Someone said it looked like an advertisement for the Smith Brothers cough drops. An example of how the media can pounce on a minor misstep by a candidate is illustrated by the extraordinary coverage given to a final press release statement that I gave the newspapers during the last week of the campaign charging Frank Newell with raiding the petty cash fund assigned to his office in order to go to a prosecuting attorney's convention in Texas. I did not charge him with anything illegal, only questioned the use of County monies for the trip. Nevertheless, both radio and newspapers gave it maximum play as if I had charged Newell with robbing the piggybank.

The 1960s were a time spent in other frenetic local, political matters. In 1960, I was chairman of a Kennedy registration drive, the purpose being to register unregistered voters in key precincts that historically had gone Democratic, i.e. in Essex and Dundalk. In 1962, I aligned with the Christian H. Kahl faction of the Democratic Party and ran for the House of Delegates when all such positions in Baltimore County were "at large," there being no legislative districts, reapportionment not having occurred.

Though an old "Pol", Chris Kahl was a very able and far-sighted leader, who campaigned for reapportionment and charter government which would bring the County into the 20th century. The primary contest became extremely bitter as the opposition headed by former County Commissioner, Michael Birmingham, had members like A. Gordon Boone, Sr., majority leader in the Maryland House of Delegates, and others implicated in our first savings and loan scandal. Campaigning meant going to meetings from as far away as Arbutus and winding up in Maryland Line or Dundalk all in one night. I took up the savings and loan theme and pounded the opposition because so many of their leading candidates were implicated. Though I led our ticket, all of us were defeated by a margin of a few thousand votes. Because of the bitterness of the campaign, a young Republican named Spiro T. Agnew picked up much of the Kahl organization in the general election and was elected County Executive on his first step towards Vice Presidency of the United States.

Though I had not campaigned for Agnew, he asked me to become replacement chairman of the County Human Relations Commission at a time when there were massive demonstrations at Gwynn Oak State Park with dozens of clergymen being arrested. I held that position from January, 1964 until the end of June, 1966, helping to keep the lid on the situation.

Our Commission obtained a rerouting of the projected road system in east Towson, which would have displaced many black families. We had regular monthly meetings and we found that if we scheduled Al Kaltenbach, head of the Dept. of Public Works or a ranking subordinate, on a periodic basis, the road alignment was consistently being changed to take fewer and fewer properties of black families in east Towson. The key was having the spotlight of media attention on our meetings.

Other duties consisted of running interference for the County Executive where racial controversy was involved. One time I had an emergency call to come to the County Office building because of fears of a violent demonstration about to occur. As I walked toward the County Executive's office, I saw police cars everywhere. The County Office building was practically barricaded. In front of it was a small group of about 12 black teenagers carrying signs – so much for the violent demonstration.

On another occasion, I was called by Agnew to represent him at the time of a Palm Sunday demonstration around the Courthouse when a group carrying a cross appeared after a long walk from the Chase area of Baltimore County. A counter-demonstration was being conducted by some neo-Nazis called the National State's Rights Party. As I walked with Chester Wickwire, the Johns Hopkins chaplain, to help him get into his car with his walking crutches, one of the State's Righters shouted "We've got your number, Iglehart! We know about AVC!" My response was "My dues are current!" Agnew was nowhere around during this encounter. He had started his political career as a Rockefeller Republican, but after the 1968 riots in Baltimore and his denunciation of the moderate black leaders on television for failure to stem the unrest, he made his alliance with Nixon and was on his way to becoming Vice President.

During my chairmanship of the Human Relations Commission, I tried to maintain close, friendly contact with the Baltimore County Chief of Police, Bob Lally, a former FBI agent. When the Baltimore riots occurred in 1968 after Martin Luther King's assassination, I found myself posting a situation map in the County Civil Defense office as part of my Army Reserve duties, an ironic take on the racial situation. After his successful election as governor in 1966, when George Mahoney's campaign slogan "Your Home is Your Castle" turned off many Democratic voters, Agnew appointed Bob Lally as State Police Chief.

After Agnew's television appearance attacking moderate black leaders referred to above, I received a call from Chief Lally, who said he was very concerned about Agnew's statement and relationship with the black community, particularly since he was supposed to give a key address at an upcoming conference of the National Association of Christians and Jews scheduled for the then Friendship Airport, and suggested that the two of us go to visit him in the governor's mansion to counsel a more moderate statement. When the day arrived for our appointment, Lally and I were ushered into the governor's office where we cooled our heels while he talked with a secretary on the intercom about some checking account and whether or not certain deposits had been made in it. Finally, turning to us, Agnew asked for the purpose of our visit and we laid it out. His response was he knew we were right in one sense, but we should look at the pile of thousands of telegrams he had received from white constituents praising him for his statement. We realized that his course was set. He was on his way to becoming a different kind of Republican. Agnew brought with him to the governor's office and later the Vice Presidency, a rather parochial form of corruption, accepting cash bribes rather than large contributions by checks.

Coinciding with my work on the Human Relations Commission was a 2 ½ year term from 1964 to June 1966 on the County Planning Board, becoming acting chairman in the last two months of my term due to the resignation of chairman, Harry Dundore, president of the Diecraft Co. The Planning Board had responsibility for proposing new forms of zoning legislation and reviewing the County budget each year. How I was able to undertake all of these activities and still practice law is beyond me. I had been acting Chairman about a week when I received a telephone call from George Gavrelis, Executive Director of the Planning Board, to say that the "boss" wanted us to vote approval of a new county dump site on property between Cuba Road and the Hunt Valley area. I told Gavrelis that the site might be a good one, but the members of the Board had not seen it or read any of the technical reports about it, all of which would have to be done first before we could possibly vote approval. It was not long before my term on the Board drew to an end, and Agnew did not ask me to serve another one.

From 1964 to 1966, I was heavily involved in the preparation and trial of two leading cases: a slip and fall case which established an important precedent on appeal, and a hotel fire case in Indiana, which I will write about later. In 1964, I helped to broker a merger of the Christian Kahl forces with the campaign of Joseph D. Tydings for the United States Senate, which was ultimately successful, Baltimore County being his best county in his race against Louis L. Goldstein, the State Comptroller. As 1966 wore on, it became time for the regular bloodletting between the two Democratic factions, and I spent much time in brokering a merger between the Kahl forces and part of the regular Democratic organization in the western area of the county in support of an unsullied candidate for County Executive, Frederick Dewberry. One night we had a meeting in Chris Kahl's office to round out the ticket starting with the position for State's Attorney. A number of names were tossed about, but each one was deemed to be lacking in political strength, though competent. Then someone mentioned the name of Samuel Green, a County Councilman who was reported to be ready to leave the regular organization and run for State's Attorney against the incumbent, Frank Newell. I opined that he would be the right candidate, having political strength and though not a brilliant lawyer, would bring no scandals to the office – a bad prediction when not long thereafter, Sam Green immersed his office in a steamy sex scandal, the details of which will not be recounted here. I ran for State Senate in a newly created legislative district and managed to run second in a field of 7. About 40% of the Kahl candidates won their positions, Dewberry losing by a few thousand votes to the organization candidate, Dale Anderson, later the subject of a different kind of scandal. All of this was going on while I was practicing law.

An outgrowth of my membership in AVC and Chairmanship of the County Human Relations Commission was the formation of a nonprofit corporation called Metro Housing, Inc. This occurred at the behest of Dr. Eugene D. Byrd, who called a meeting at his house one evening in 1968 when the riots in Baltimore were raging and fires burning everywhere. Gene Byrd said we had an obligation to do something positive and the general consensus was that it should be in the housing field. Gene Byrd provided the inspiration, but I wound up doing most of the work primarily because the Human Relations Commissioner gave me a good understanding of the housing situation in east Towson where there was inadequate housing for black families who had been the residents in the area for several centuries.

A site was acquired through laborious negotiations conducted with the president of the American Totalisator Company which donated some spare land to add to lots that we acquired from families in the area, the plan being to create a Section 8, subsidized rental housing project, the first in Baltimore County. Metro Housing's Board included Dr. Byrd, myself, Bob Hendrickson on staff of the City Housing authority, and Iona McQuay, a prominent east Towson civic leader. The practical implementation of our general plan came in the person of a young employee in the Knott organization named Larry Thanner, who had recently left them and was looking for a Section 8 project that he could be successful with. He obtained the private investors who put up the funds to reimburse Metro Housing for the monies outlaid to acquire the parcels of land and handled the necessary paperwork with HUD. The result was a 29 unit development which we named McQuay Homes after Iona's death. A photograph of the groundbreaking ceremony is shown on page 85 with Don Hutchison, then County Executive, Barbara Bachur, Councilwoman, Dr. Eugene Byrd, Reverend McManus, and myself. The project was completed in 1981. The funds provided by Thanner's private investors were later used to acquire additional lots next to the Mt. Calvary AME Church, later donated to the church for its expansion to become a true community center adjacent to the housing project with provision for an adequate daycare center and other amenities.

The mention of Don Hutchison reminds me of other activities. In 1974 and 1975, I became the default Chairman of a State legislative task force to deal with the issue of public funding of political campaigns. The membership of the task force was 50% elected officials and 50% citizenry. George Solter was expected to be Chairman but he opted out, and I wound up taking his place, working closely with Don Hutchison, a member of the House of Delegates from Essex, during sessions that lasted over a two year period with absolutely no tangible result. Nevertheless, when Don became County Executive, he backed Jimmy Carter in the 1976 campaign and asked me to run as a candidate for convention delegate, which I did, and was easily elected: the only election I ever won. The convention in New York City was pretty boring and my chief memory of that time is riding downtown with Don who was describing the one woman performance by Julie Harris in the "Belle of Amherst" that he and his wife had seen the night before, an unusual interest for a politician, but he had been an English major at Frostburg State College. However, I am getting ahead of my story and should return to the law.

Groundbreaking Ceremony
l.to r. F.N. Iglehart, Rev. McManus, Don Hutchinson,
Barbara Bachur, and Dr. Eugene Byrd

CHAPTER 15
SLIP AND FALL

In 1964, an elderly, Quaker lady named Mrs. Taylor was ascending a steep stairway from the parking garage area at the Hutzler Brothers department store in Towson. Upon reaching the top step, she lost her balance when her foot went into a depression in the sidewalk and she fell fracturing her ankle, followed several weeks later by a pulmonary thrombosis.

The legal issues in the case concerned whether or not Mrs. Taylor was guilty of contributory negligence in not avoiding the depression in the sidewalk, and whether she was or was not a business invitee of Hutzler Brothers as she readily conceded that she had not intended to go shopping there where she had parked her car, intending instead to go north to the mall called Towson Plaza. Through a great deal of diligent discovery work necessitated by the evasive tactics of defense counsel, I obtained the agreement between the Towson Plaza mall management and Hutzler Brothers which gave the customers for each reciprocal privileges for parking. The case went to trial before Walter M. Jenifer, one of the very best of the Circuit Court judges despite an occasional drinking problem.

I skirted the contributory negligence problem by delicately pointing out Mrs. Taylor's girth at 168 lbs. and the fact that one's normal gaze was not down towards one's feet when walking, but straight ahead. Because of the evidence of the reciprocal parking agreement, Judge Jenifer instructed the jury *as a matter of law* that Mrs. Taylor was a business invitee of Hutzler Brothers regardless of the fact that she was not planning to purchase anything there on the particular day in question.

The jury brought in a plaintiff's verdict of $10,000 which seemed low at the time, though adequate. Defense counsel appealed primarily because of Judge Jenifer's instruction on the law, and we prevailed again on appeal. It was a lot of very hard work for a modest result. Nevertheless, it was a pleasure to try a case before Judge Jenifer.

CHAPTER 16
THE HILLSIDE HOTEL FIRE

In 1964, I was in a small partnership with Herbert M. Brune and Harrison M. Robertson with an associate, W. Holland Wilmer. I normally used our Towson office space as my base. Harrison was very successful in handling litigation involving minority stockholders causes of action. Herbert had been the author of a handbook on Maryland corporation law. My assumed forte was personal injury work and workmen's compensation.

Accordingly, one day Harrison said he wanted me to prepare a workmen's compensation death claim for a young widow named Norma Brown, whose late husband had been employed by the Davison Chemical Company and killed in a hotel fire in Indiana while on a sales trip, leaving a young widow and three small children. Norma Brown came to the office with a large folder in which were many clippings from Indiana newspapers which had given extensive coverage to the fire that totally consumed the Hillside Hotel on the north bank of the Ohio River in southern Indiana. After explaining to Norma Brown what benefits she could receive from a workmen's compensation claim, I asked her if she could leave the newspaper clippings with me to review, primarily out of curiosity. I explained to her that as a widow she had coverage under the Maryland workmen's compensation statute in that her husband was on a sales trip at the time, and therefore on duty when he lost his life in the fire.

Later that day, with nothing more pressing to do, I started reading the clippings, the most extensive coverage being in the local newspaper of Madison, Indiana where the Hillside Hotel was located. The first account caught my interest and I re-read it several times with growing wonderment. It included an interview with the hotel night clerk, who said that he smelled smoke and heard a crackling sound in the small hours of the morning and rushed across the lobby to activate the fire alarm consisting of a horn on the outside of the building. This seemed to be a rather hap-hazard way to have the occupants of the building notified of a fire. Another clipping gave the opinion of the town fire marshal, endorsed by the Indiana state fire marshal, that the fire had started in the decedent's room, the inference being that he had fallen asleep while smoking in bed pleasantly inebriated.

My curiosity being aroused, I telephoned the Maryland State Fire Marshal and told him that I was investigating a fire in Indiana and wondered if he could recommend a competent investigator. He said there were two people that he could think of. One was the famed, oil well fire trouble-shooter, "Red" Adair and a retired, West Virginia state police arson investigator who had a key role at the Curtis Bay Coast Guard training center during World War II with regard to fire control. The fire marshal said that Adair would cost $40,000-$50,000 upfront and that the West Virginia arson investigator, Lloyd Layman, could be hired for his expenses only and a liberal supply of bourbon whiskey in the course of his work. With some concern about the bourbon, I contacted Lloyd Layman at his home in Parkersburg, West Virginia.

As things unfolded, I learned more about Lloyd, who had had an extraordinary military career in a machine gun company in World War I. He had later joined the West Virginia National Guard, which acted as a strike breaking force in the coal mine wars of the 1920s. From there he went into the West Virginia state police and wound up as head of the arson squad. During World War II at the Curtis Bay Coast Guard facility, he had developed the fog nozzle technique for controlling fires. Layman expressed an interest in the case and we made arrangements for him to join me on a westbound B&O train a week later. The B&O night train didn't pull into Parkersburg until about 2 in the morning and I was a bit concerned as to what I saw. Lloyd Layman was in his middle 70s, somewhat stooped from arthritis, lean and lanky, with bushy white eyebrows and somewhat bloodshot eyes.

We got off the train at a town in southern Indiana not too far from Madison and rented a car. Layman insisted that our first objective should be the local newspaper as the fire would have been a major event in a small Indiana town. On arrival at the offices of the local newspaper, we identified ourselves as insurance investigators, and Lloyd said that we would like to look at the photographs taken of the fire. We were introduced to their young photographer, who had taken literally hundreds of shots. The hotel had been a frame structure perched on a steep hillside overlooking the Ohio River and many of the photos had been taken below the hotel looking upwards. One in particular attracted Layman's attention. It appeared to show fire in a room on the first floor at the southwest corner of the building. The young photographer said it was the very first of the several hundred that he had taken upon arriving at the scene with the first fire unit. Layman ordered a print from the negative.

Our next stop was the local radio station where the DJ obligingly played for us a tape of an interview with the night clerk while the fire was still burning. He gave the same account of having rushed across the lobby to turn on the fire siren. Following that, we went to the fire site where a young man was operating a bulldozer grading the ruins. Layman hailed him for a bit of conversation, noting that his name was the same as that of the town fire marshal, whose opinion had fixed the beginning of the fire on the second floor on the northeast corner of the building where the decedent had his room. "Yes," the young man acknowledged, "that's my Dad. We have the contract to rebuild the hotel." Mental bells started ringing. The young bulldozer operator explained that his father was a full-time building contractor and a part-time fire marshal.

Upon returning home, I called the late Max Israelson, local dean of personal injury lawyers who had served on the national board of the American Trial Lawyers Association. I explained that I was looking for a competent trial lawyer in Indiana to act as local counsel in the case. He recommended Howard Young of Indianapolis, who had served with him on the national board. I promptly dispatched a letter to Young, who called me up within several days and said that he had read about the case and, in his opinion, we didn't stand a chance in view of the fire marshal's opinion. I told him of the night clerk's statement and what the early fire photograph showed relative to fire location at the outset of the blaze. He said he would give it a second look and get back to me, which he later did having been convinced it was a case worth investigating. We later determined that the hotel had no sprinkler system, no automatic fire alarm system, and no fire doors. Suit was filed in Federal court in the southern district of Indiana in a town called New Albany across the Ohio River from Louisville.

The next order of business was the taking of depositions. We were able to obtain the scorched remains of the hotel register from which we ascertained the names and addresses of many of the occupants on the night of the fire, including those in the room where the fire first appeared in the photo series taken by the young photographer.

We had ascertained that an extensive addition had been put on the hotel's south side to create a dining room overlooking the river in the year before the fire, and we were able to obtain the architect's plans for the entire building. As depositions went forward, using the hotel register, we deposed occupants of the hotel the night of the fire from distances as far as Atlanta, Georgia; Houston, Texas; and an Army arsenal in New Jersey establishing that the first awareness of fire was below the first floor room on the southwest side of the building, which was immediately above the kitchen and smoke ducts from the stoves - about as far away from Mr. Brown's room as was possible.

Howard Young had a friend who was a model maker work from the hotel plans to create a model with rooms to which numbers could be assigned. He said that our case was important enough to have a complete investigation done of the jury panel, the results of which were not very encouraging. The investigator reported that the prospective juror who was most likely to be an ally was the town alcoholic and that the median income of the entire group was very low. New Albany was a poor cousin to Louisville across the river and the courtroom was as shabby as many of the houses in the town.

We went to trial two years after the fire with Lloyd Layman and a friend who was an expert in fire codes in attendance. Howard Young handled the liability aspect of the case whereas I concentrated on testimony that would establish the value of the decedent's life, his future prospects with the Davison Chemical Company, etc. The defense asserted that the hotel conformed with the local fire code by being "grandfathered" from the requirements of the more modern code. Our planned counter-attack was case law to show that the modern code could be held up as an example of a proper standard of care. The clincher was that the addition put on by the part-time, town fire marshal was erected in a timeframe that brought it under the modern fire code. As trial testimony progressed, some of it being read from depositions, we were able to pinpoint the location of occupants with the use of Howard's model. The night clerk told his tale again for the umpteenth time in which he helpfully explained that the siren he turned on was a civil defense siren installed during World War II, and that there were no sprinklers, no fire doors, etc.

On the third day of trial, defense counsel signaled that they wanted a recess in order to discuss settlement, which, of course, the presiding judge granted. We huddled in a spare conference room with the attorney for the insurance carrier and the hotel owners' personal attorney. It had been a Mom & Pop operation, and the only coverage they had was for $200,000 for all occurrences, possibly worth four times that today. The judge allowed the case to recess for the rest of the day, so that Howard and I could talk to Norma Brown explaining to her that we had an offer of policy limits and that looked as if that was all we could get. It was a bitter pill - in fact, wormwood and gall considering the potential value of the case with a young widow and three children surviving, but we appeared to have no choice and she acquiesced.

Back in court, the judge explained to the jury that the case had been settled and thanked them for their efforts. As they left the jury box, the number 12 juror, a big, burly retired locomotive engineer wearing red suspenders announced in a loud tone of voice that he didn't see why that fellow (meaning Brown) couldn't have gotten out of his room in time to avoid being burned to death. Howard and I looked at each other and agreed that we had been lucky to have settled.

I still have a framed copy of the photograph taken by the young photographer marked as a deposition exhibit hanging in my conference room. When Lloyd Layman died they had a memorial symposium in his honor at the Emmitsburg National Fire Safety Center where I was asked to speak and told the audience the story of the hotel fire that had been solved by Lloyd Layman who worked for expenses only and that occasional bottle of bourbon.

Howard Young, Esq.
Indianapolis, Indiana

Hillside Hotel
Deposition Exhibit

CHAPTER 17
ASSUMPTION OF THE RISK

Not long after the conclusion of the Hillside Hotel fire case, I was heavily involved in an unusual personal injury case with an attorney from Rockville named R. Edwin Brown with whom our senior partner, Herbert Brune, had a number of matters over the years. Ed Brown had a client named James Lawrence who was a poor farm-hand employed by a wealthy, real estate developer to manage one of the many farms that he had acquired for development in Montgomery County. There was still a dairy herd on the place, and it was Lawrence's job to take care of the entire herd, rising at 4 in the morning to start the milking process. His only access to the barn to throw down hay was on a nearby wooden ladder about which he complained to his employer, David Cavanagh, deeming it to be unsafe.

According to the testimony, Cavanagh assured him that he would get him a modern aluminum ladder at some point in time but never did. Eventually, one of the rungs broke under Lawrence's weight and he fell to the ground rupturing a lumbar disk with a substantial partial disability.

Ed Brown's forte was condemnation cases representing landowners. Given the expansion of mass transit lines in the Washington area, it was a fertile field to work in and he had won many large awards for clients. Recognizing the problems in the case arising from the doctrine of assumption of the risk, he contacted me to help him prepare and try the case in a manner that would get us over the legal hurdle of assumption of the risk. The division of labor was that I examined all the witnesses, took pretrial depositions, prepared the legal briefs with regard to what the defense would rely on, and Ed Brown handled opening and closing arguments to the jury.

The case was tried at the right time of year for a plaintiff, i.e. only about 10 days before Christmas in 1966, concluding on December 14 after 3 days. Jim Lawrence presented a sympathetic picture to the jury, having been reduced to part-time work as a school janitor, and Ed Brown pulled out all the stops before the jury in opening and closing arguments - truly a virtuoso performance. I had prepared a Memorandum of Law in advance to counter the expected defendant's motion to take the case from the jury and Judge John Moore agreed with our theories that assumption of the risk, even in such an extreme situation, was a matter for the jury to decide.

It was 5 pm on a late December afternoon when Ed Brown and I walked down the hill to his office with the understanding that the judge's bailiff would call us if and when the jury returned a verdict. We had no more finished putting our feet up on his conference table and started sipping cups of coffee when the telephone rang. The jury was back. We trudged up the hill feeling totally defeated because to have a jury come back so quickly could only mean a defendant's verdict. To our astonishment, the foreman read the verdict of $50,000 causing James Couch, our opponent, to jump to his feet and exclaim "Jesus Christ!" and then apologize to the court for his outburst. Jim Lawrence's "specials", i.e. medical expenses and other out of pocket losses, were less than $2,000. Ed Brown huddled immediately with Lawrence and his wife and told them whatever they did, not to buy anything on the assumption that the verdict would stand because there would be an appeal beyond question.

In due course, defense counsel filed a motion *non obstante veredicto*, or for a new trial, and on April 13, 1967 reversing his trial position, Judge Moore granted the motion and we appealed. Lawrence ignored the advice given to him and entered into a contract for the purchase of a new home. I was later pleased and gratified when defense counsel made an offer of $15,000 on the strength of our appeal brief, tracking my prior submission to Judge Moore, but Lawrence said that he had been given an award by a jury of his peers and it was his right as an American citizen to have his rights decided by a jury not by a bunch of lawyers and judges. It was too much assumption of the risk for the Court of Appeals to swallow, and we lost our appeal. I always thought that if our verdict had not been so large, we would have had an entirely different outcome.

CHAPTER 18
1968

Though the subject matter of this chapter would logically fall in with the prior chapter titled "Other Activities", I have devoted a separate placement for it because the year 1968 has always seemed to me to be a watershed in the history of the country. As a result of what happened in the presidential election, from my perspective, it led to a much prolonged war in Vietnam and the Watergate scandal.

I was asked to head up an "organization" called Citizens for Humphrey-Muskie. I am not entirely sure as to who did the asking. Apparently the genesis of the Citizens concept lay with Jerry Hoffberger, his brother-in-law, Irv Blum, and Edgar Berman, who was Hubert Humphrey's personal physician. Bob Smelkinson's wife, Jackie Smelkinson, a gadfly political activist, was brought into the discussions with these prominent Democrats and she may have suggested me. I may have been acceptable because of my former role in the 1964 Tydings campaign and chairmanship of the County Human Relations Commission, Planning Board, etc.

The first effort on the part of Citizens for Humphrey-Muskie was the arrangements for a concert to be given by Frank Sinatra at the Civic Center with the proceeds being donated for the campaign. The concert was a smashing success and close to $50,000 was netted from Sinatra's performance. Of course this was long before he and the rest of the "Rat Pack" shifted to the other side politically. The amount of money on hand promptly precipitated a battle over control of the funds. I was summoned to the downtown office of Maryland Attorney General, Francis "Bill" Burch, and was told that the proceeds should go the Democratic State Central Committee for disbursement as they saw fit in the general election. I demurred and said that it was obviously earmarked for the presidential campaign only, and Burch's somewhat angry response was that I and my committee was nothing but a figment of someone's imagination. Marvin Mandel was present smoking his pipe with a Chesire cat-like countenance and said nothing. The upshot was that we kept the money and it was used for salaries of people like Jackie Smelkinson, who ran the operation, mass mailings and other expenses. Part of the operation was the laborious scanning of names of registered voters in the city and the surrounding metropolitan area for anyone with a Polish sounding name to whom a letter was sent on behalf of the Senator Ed Muskie. There was also a major effort to get out the black vote.

The National party had employed a New York advertising agency that was preparing radio and tv spots for the election. One that I remember vividly had someone with a Brooklyn accent denouncing rednecks in the south who might be voting for Nixon. I wired the Democratic National Committee chairman and suggested that the ad and similar ones be pulled. After all, there were a lot of rednecks in Maryland. As a result, I got a wire in reply giving me authority over all media advertising in the state. I felt rather heady about that.

Because of the fractured state of the Democratic party as a result of Eugene McCarthy's anti-war campaign and all those who were ready to support Bobby Kennedy prior to his assassination, we thought it important to get prominent local Kennedy and McCarthy supporters to "walk the plank" before television cameras and get their endorsement for Humphrey and Muskie. We had several such sessions before our headquarters in the 400 block of North Charles Street and I am sure they made a great difference. By contrast, in the state of the California the Democratic party never did get itself together. A McCarthy supporter was arrested for throwing a rock through our headquarter's bay window; but we declined to prosecute as part of our inclusive strategy.

Ed Muskie came to town towards the end of September, and there was a big affair at the Polish hall on lower Broadway followed by a victory parade to Patterson Park. It was one of those luminous September days when you feel that all is right with the world and that your side is bound to win. In fact, as the campaign drew to a close we began to feel better and better about the prospects, at least in Maryland. Wallace Lanahan phoned in to say that he had just gotten a cab to go to the Maryland Club and the driver had told him that he was sure that Humphrey and Muskie would prevail. On the strength of that statement, Wallace said that he was sending us a check for $1,000 more. In the end, despite all the horrors that occurred in Chicago, Nixon lost Maryland by approximately 20,000 votes. Nationally, Humphrey lost by about the same margin that Gore had in the popular vote over Bush. On election night, I went to the hotel where the regular pols were gathered and had a brief conversation with Marvin Mandel, who said that without our operation we wouldn't have prevailed in Maryland. It may be simply an article of faith, but I remain convinced that if Humphrey had won, there would have been no bombing of Hanoi and a much earlier end to the war in Vietnam.

CHAPTER 19
ZONING MAPS

Under Baltimore County zoning law, the zoning of every property within the county is reviewed by the County Council every four years, the first review occurring in 1970-71. Because of my membership on the County Planning Board until June 1966, I was assumed to have some expertise in zoning law, and was contacted by Steve Sachs, former U.S. Attorney for Maryland, to work with him as local counsel in representing property owners, mostly physicians in the Ruxton/Old Court Road area, who were greatly concerned by the Rouse Company plans to re-zone the Johnson property on Falls Road immediately south of the gateway to the Greenspring Valley for a massive commercial and condominium development which would be reminiscent of Cross Keys. Steve said "Iglehart, you handle the law, and I'll collect the fees from the clients."

Aside from the raw politics of the proceedings, the only law that was involved was preparation of a Memorandum that would be presented to the 7 members of the County Council so that if there was a later challenge to the zoning they enacted, they could refer to the Memorandum and testify that they had not acted arbitrarily but after due consideration of all the factors involved. The Johnson property was divided into the areas of Councilman Gary Huddles, later convicted in another zoning imbroglio, and

Jack Tyrie, head of a tombstone company in Cockeysville. They were heavily lobbied by our side and even wined and dined at the home of a prominent surgeon and his wife. The Rouse company pulled out all the stops in their campaign for the required zoning with speakers at every local improvement association meeting for months. It was the only time that I can recall where the protestants were classified as "the bad guys" for opposing the sanctified Rouse Company whose plans for Columbia had received favorable publicity throughout the country.

The Council vote went in our favor, and the Johnson property is still relatively open land. I drafted and filed a learned memorandum of law ending with a flourish referring to Samuel Butler's utopian novel "Erehwon" (nowhere spelled backwards) stating that the Rouse Company's designs would put principles of planning in a conceptual erehwon. The harassed typist translated this arcane reference as putting the principles of zoning "in concept's pond." I didn't catch the error until after the memorandum had been filed and called up Steve Sachs to suggest that we file an amendment. He roared with laughter and said "No, let it stand. Let's see if anybody on the Council notices it." None did.

CHAPTER 20
THE RAINMAKER

Through Herbert Brune, my senior partner, I was engaged to represent a former Georgia sharecropper's son who had first worked as a page in the House of Representatives and became known in Washington as a first-rate influence peddler. His name was Myrvin Clark and he had been indicted in Federal court in Baltimore for conspiracy to commit mail fraud in conjunction with an east Texas Congressman named John Dowdy. Dowdy was the main goal of the Feds and Myrvin was used to apply leverage against him. Prosecuting the case in Baltimore was Stephen Sachs, former US Attorney for Maryland, who was asked to stay on to prosecute the case by the Republican administration. All this was before the zoning map case.

The operation that had been under investigation by the FBI was a so-called home improvement company in Washington that sold contracts to poor, black homeowners and altered the figures to increase the contract price and often foreclosed the phony mortgages. As the FHA and other agencies began to investigate the company due to the countless complaints against it, Myrvin raised the sum of $25,000 from the principals in the company and delivered the amount in cash to Congressman Dowdy at the Atlanta airport as an investment for protection against future investigations. In 1971, Dowdy was indicted by a grand jury in Baltimore for mail fraud, conspiracy, etc. and Myrvin was indicted for conspiracy.

Through Steve Sachs, I was notified that the FBI wanted to interrogate our client and I was permitted to sit in on the whipsawing of Myrvin by two FBI agents over the course of 7-8 hours. To apply further pressure to him, Myrvin was indicted in the District of Columbia, and the deal was that if Myrvin became a government witness against Dowdy, things would go easy for him at the time of sentencing.

The day came for Myrvin's arraignment in D.C. He had been sequestered in the Lord Baltimore Hotel and an FBI agent was to see that he had no alcohol. I got up at the crack of dawn to be at the hotel a little after 7 am to drive him to the District for the arraignment and found out to my horror that there was an empty bottle of vodka on the table by his bed. His bloodshot eyes told the rest of the story. A busboy had been bribed to bring him the booze. Somehow I got him dressed and a few cups of coffee in him and we drove off for the District.

When we arrived at court, I nervously glanced at my client who appeared to have a long way to go before becoming completely sober. The presiding judge interrogated him as to his state of mind in entering a guilty plea, going through the usual rigamorale about making the decision without undue pressure or promises from the government. When the time came for the fundamental question as to whether he was under the influence of drugs or alcohol, the question was worded in such a way that he was able to respond in the negative. If the question had been rephrased to ask if he had had consumed anything in the last 24 hours, the answer would have been different.

For the tactical reasons, it was decided to try Congressman Dowdy in the US District Court in Baltimore where he was convicted and sentenced. There was a long hiatus during which time Myrvin and his family were stashed out of sight under the government's witness protection program in a strange place called California City about 100 miles east of Los Angeles in the middle of the desert. Harriet and I had occasion to go to California to visit our eldest daughter and I decided it would be interesting to see Myrvin in this place called California City. We drove down the coast stopping at places like Santa Barbara and then drove into the desert where we occasionally saw signs advertising a Holiday Inn in California City to the east. There was indeed a Holiday Inn in California City but that was about all, there being perhaps not more than 20 or 30 houses surrounded by desert and mesquite. It was the California version of the old Florida land boom technique. People were being sold quarter-acre lots on the strength of advertising to show the Holiday Inn and adjacent lake. The water table was being constantly lowered by tapping the aquifers for water for the development. Half of the time of the visit with Myrvin and family was spent in prayer meetings with him and certain friends that he made there. The visit gave me the opportunity to take my first ever glider flights upon release from a tow plane operating out of the Mojave airport. There wasn't much else to do in California City.

When the time came for Dowdy's trial in Baltimore, Myrvin was brought in under wraps and when the day came for his appearance, I sat in the back of Judge Rosczel Thomson's courtroom to hear the testimony. Before Myrvin testified, Judge Thomson addressed a question to me to ask if I had advised him of his rights or words to that effect. The result was Dowdy's conviction and a suspended sentence for Myrvin. In 1976 with all the celebrations of the Bicentennial year in D.C., Myrvin saw a good thing and began promoting a so-called Indian tribe and its "chief" with all kinds of memorabilia for the occasion. He was truly a rainmaker – a promoter in a class by himself.

Mojave Desert-1975

CHAPTER 21
DEATH OF A CHILD

In 1973, tragedy struck my own family. My nephew's child, little Bobby, was in a cotton bathrobe at his home when his mother heard him screaming and found that he had run upstairs from the first floor with the robe engulfed in flames, causing third degree burns over 75% of his body. He survived for 6 weeks with his father going to see him for hours everyday while trying to run a small business. Bobby's death was followed by his father's death from a heart attack a few weeks later. He had had rheumatic fever as a child and was not in the best of health. The strain and anguish of what had happened was too much for him to bear.

One day I was reading the American Trial Lawyers regular newsletter and noted a reference to an attorney in Providence, Rhode Island named Leonard Decof, who had obtained a large award by persuading a court that a proposed clothing flammability protection regulation could be introduced into evidence as a standard of care even where a particular fabric "passed" the requirements of the existing regulation. My initial moral dilemma was whether to persuade Bobby's mother to pursue the route of litigation with all of the stress that that would entail with the reopening of terrible wounds, or to break new ground in law and establish a case precedent that might ultimately save other children.

Bobby's mother said to go ahead and I flew to Providence to meet with Leonard Decof, a short, wiry man who had established a substantial personal injury practice, including aircraft litigation, flammable fabrics, and other areas of the law. Leonard was the son of a New York City cabdriver and had won a scholarship to Yale where he was a very lightweight quarterback on the football team. He knew the route to take with the case and agreed to join me which lifted a great personal burden from my shoulders as he would provide completely independent judgment about the merits of what we were doing.

Suit was filed in the United States District Court for the District of Maryland against the vendor of the bathrobe, the McCrory Corporation and other defendants under diversity of citizenship. Our expert witness was a Dr. Beroes, a chemical engineer on the faculty of the University of Pittsburgh who had testified in many such cases using a small glass enclosed chamber to measure the rapidity of burning time of different types of fabric. The case was assigned to Judge Joseph Young on the Federal bench and in a pre-trial conference, he indicated that he would permit a small controlled burning experiment to be done by Dr. Beroes in court.

To our astonishment later when the trial began, as Leonard Decof was making his opening statement telling the jury that we would have the burning experiment done in court, Judge Young interjected "Not in my court you won't." Leonard recovered nimbly and finished his opening statement, but it was downhill from there on with countless evidentiary rulings against us. In addition, defense counsel behaved abominably, treating the case with unseemly levity and insinuating in cross-examination of Bobby's mother that she was responsible for his death by allowing him to light candles on a birthday cake shortly before the accident. After a two week trial, we wound up with a hung jury and under Federal Rule 59, Judge Young granted a motion to dismiss the case for lack of evidence of violation of a standard of care as he ruled that Dr. Beroes had gone beyond his area of expertise and given testimony as if he were a safety engineer.

I handled the appeal to the Fourth Circuit Court of Appeals in Richmond, did the brief and argued the case before a three judge panel there on October 2, 1978. The suit had originally been docketed in December, 1973. The Fourth Circuit decision was issued on June 13, 1979 reversing Judge Young and holding that lay testimony alone might be sufficient for a jury to consider whether an inherently dangerous product was involved or not, the case being remanded for re-trial.

Leonard Decof congratulated me on the result, but said that I had to do whatever might be necessary to get Judge Young off the case, a prospect I did not particularly relish. Bobby's mother said that she would not go back to court before Judge Young under any circumstances whatsoever. That was something that we had to keep from the knowledge of the other side. I finally decided to prepare a Memorandum citing about a dozen different evidentiary rulings that Young had made which were so blatantly erroneous or prejudicial that the Memorandum concluded by saying that the plaintiff, Bobby's mother, did not feel she could have fair trial before this particular member of the bench. This Memorandum was filed with a motion for recusal and we waited weeks with no response from the court until one day a letter came from my old friend from Isadore and Natalie's divorce case, Judge Shirley Jones, who had received a lateral appointment to the Federal bench from the Supreme bench of Baltimore City. The letter said that as counsel may know, the case had been transferred to her for re-trial. A major blow in our favor!

In a pre-trial conference, Judge Jones indicated that she would permit the burning time experiment to be performed in open court by Dr. Beroes. Though the Fourth Circuit had ruled that lay testimony alone might be sufficient in such a case to establish the issue of an inherently dangerous product, I thought we might tighten the case up considerably by getting further expert testimony on the rapidity of ignition. Shaw Wilgis, the eminent hand surgeon who had treated me at one time or another, recommended Dr. Andrew Munster, the head of the burn unit at City Hospital, a well known Australian surgeon whom I met with at length. He had statistical analyses of ignition time for different products, including the type of cotton used in Bobby's bathrobe, showing that ignition and third-degree burns could occur within less than one second in the case of vertical burning. We notified defense counsel that we had a new expert witness on this point and identified the Australian doctor. Not long thereafter, the case was settled for a six figure sum.

I like to think that I recommended the correct course of action since the case did create an appellate decision that would be important in future flammable fabrics cases, or other cases where fire was the cause of injury or death.

CHAPTER 22
DOGBITE LITIGATION

In the early 1970s, J. Michael McLaughlin became an associate and I promptly put him to work in a dogbite case. The clients' five year old child had climbed down a pair of cellar steps to a landing where a large St. Bernard dog was lying asleep. The child pounced on the dog, who reacted quickly and violently, biting him about the face and head inflicting injuries that required over 50 sutures to close. The benign personality attributed to St. Bernards in the popular mind made it important to determine whether he had ever bitten without warning before. Michael became candidate for the chief investigator and was dispatched to the Essex area where the dog's owners lived. He proceed to knock on many doors and hit a jackpot in finding a couple who had encountered the dog not many months before, ending not only in a bite that required tetanus inoculation but impoundment and observation for rabies at a local veterinary hospital.

In order to maintain maximum advantage at trial, we withheld information about the prior dogbite and the main issue at trial appeared to be that of liability. With the effect on the child as a result of the bite emerging as a larger and larger issue since we had testimony from his pediatrician that he was beginning to act very hyper, and becoming very unruly in elementary school, the defense had retained an eminent child neurologist, R.M. Crosby, a neighbor of mine and fellow parishioner, whose written reports gave the opinion that the child's hyperactivity would have occurred regardless of the dogbite. To save the expense of a deposition, I obtained an agreement with defense counsel to interview Dr. Crosby on this point and concluded after an hour of careful review of the case with him in his office, that he would be a formidable adversary as a witness even though we had obtained maximum surprise and jury effect with the production of the local Essex veterinarian's records that proved beyond doubt that the dog had been a menace before. We recommended, and the clients agreed, to settlement for considerably less than we had originally looked for. The case illustrated how a secondary issue in a case can become the primary issue, and that one needed to remain very versatile as a trial attorney.

CHAPTER 23
HORSES AGAIN

After hospitalization for polio, I really did not start riding seriously again for a period of 6 or 7 years. My left leg was quite weak, but I managed more or less with a balancing act. In the 1960s, I had begun foxhunting regularly again, participating in old-fashioned cross-country races. One of the best horses I ever had was a loaner from the Santoro family, a mare named Worth the Price, nicknamed "Worthless," that they had bred down in the Middleburg area and brought with them to Maryland when they moved up. This was the same period of time when I was heavily involved in local politics with the Chris Kahl faction in 1962 and 1966.

From 1964 to 1966, I was Chairman of the County Human Relations Commission and somehow managed to find time to practice law, including the preparation and trial of the slip and fall case on the Hutzler Brothers' walkway and the hotel fire case in Indiana. I guess that's why I came up with this title's reference to being an "occasional attorney."

The horse that stands out the most in my mind we acquired from Kitty Jenkins, MFH of the Greenspring Valley Hunt Club. He was a big 16-hand 2 failed flat horse, being too big for the turns at the track. By Piano Jim out of Maryland Miss, he was named Maryland Jim. Kitty's daughter, Louisa, was hunting him regularly and gave me a cross-country try-out on him as she accompanied on another horse and I was sold. Later we were told the Jenkins family disliked the horse intensely because of certain mannerisms such as violently shying at such things as birds flying out of bushes. This caused me to break several fingers on one hand as a result of standing up in the stirrups while trotting along with my hand resting on the horse's mane.

Nevertheless, most of the time he could really run and jump, and as I approached my 50th year, I thought the time had come to give it a try again, only more deliberately and carefully than I had campaigned with General many years before. I persuaded our neighbor, Tom Voss, later to become the leading steeplechase trainer in the U.S., to take him as a project. I did a lot of the schooling and galloping under Tom's tutelage, but prudently decided I would get someone else to ride him in his first timber race. The person I selected was Johnny Bosley, an accomplished though sometimes controversial horseman.

The debut was to be the Elkridge-Harford Races on the Voss Atlanta Hall Farm. I told Johnny just to give him a school and not to push him. As the field rounded the barns where there was a substantial fence on the backside of the course, Jim decided that a person standing on the wings of the fence with a long telephoto lens was a threatening figure and did a 90 degree refusal, causing Johnny to go sailing through the air and suffer a quite hard fall. While the others

121

went on, he retrieved the horse, remounted, and when the field went by a second time, joined back in the race, jumping well and finishing third or fourth, though the stewards were outraged at Johnny Bosley's flouting of all the rules.

We entered him in the Rappahannock Races and Johnny had a commanding lead about 12 lengths in front of the next horse going into the last fence when he raised his bat to get the proverbial "Big One," which caused Jim to do another 90 degrees with Johnny sailing through the air. This time he did not remount. I persuaded him to try Jim one more time for both of their sakes and he ran well in a 12 horse field at Fair Hill, finishing about fifth, though quite tired on a very hot Memorial Day.

I decided that the safest way to ride Jim in a race was not to ask him for a "Big One" and to leave the bat behind. The following year, the time came for me to ride him at Rappahannock. As we lined up waiting for the flag to drop, I was distinctly aware of a pounding, drumming sound which I later realized was blood pounding in my ears, not the sound of the horse's hooves as we took off. All went well as we vied for the lead, head and head with a horse named Boca Bird. The Rappahannock course is very hilly with a very steep downgrade preceded by a very steep upgrade. The second time around, Jim decided he didn't like what he was doing and I had to kick him over the last three fences finishing dead last and somewhat embarrassed.

The culmination of all this two year effort was entering him in Tiger Bennett's little Deer Creek National Steeplechase, a very informal local event over a course that I had laid out myself with Mr. Bennett. My former jockey, Johnny Bosley, was riding a horse for one of his owners named Shalimar Blue. Doug Verzi, who owned and operated the auto body shop in Madonna, was on a mare that very soon ran off course and was not seen again for some time. Johnny and I competed together jumping the final fence head and head and Jim outbumped his horse in the stretch as I went to bat with my right hand. It was a splendid half-length victory memorialized in a photograph of the last fence which hangs in the old living room. The year was 1980 and I had turned 55.

As I look back, Maryland Jim still stands out as a favorite horse and it was with the greatest regret when we had to put him down several years ago due to extreme decrepitude. He is buried in a special place next to our wildflower bed. He had a certain quirky personality which kept you on your toes while mounted. However, for foxhunting, an occasional timber race, and team events, he was a lot of horse. When he was right, he was really right.

Though Maryland Jim was a big horse, size was not the key. Much smaller horses showed lots of heart. One that I hunted when Jim began to go seriously lame was a little horse named Drummer. One day we had a joint meet with Bob Crompton's pack of hounds in the Unionville, Pennsylvania area and I remember that in the course of a 2 ½ hour run we jumped 33 fences including a full size farm gate. I could not do that today for sure.

In 1985, Doug Small, who had taken over the job of hunting the Elkridge-Harford hounds due to the legendary Dallas Leith's age and infirmity, decided it was time for him to retire as joint MFH. That would have left Eleanor Tydings Schapiro ("Ellie") and Martha Symington Sanger ("Marty") as joints. Due to an apparently erroneous belief that it was essential to have a male on the team, I was drafted to join them and lasted for 10 years. It was a time of transition, somewhat difficult in many respects. Mary Lee Atkinson, who was a protégé of Dallas Leith, the great huntsman from Virginia, had taken over successfully hunting hounds at the suggestion of Doug Small. However, the handwriting was on the wall, namely that the Whipper-In that we had hired from Mrs. Hannum's club in Unionville, Pennsylvania, Geoff Hyde, would eventually take over, which he did. This created considerable tension and there were two schools of foxhunters in the Club, those who favored Mary Lee, and those who wanted to really run and jump who favored Geoff.

During much of this time, I hunted a very large beast named Skaneatles, all of 17 hands 2 inches but beautifully proportioned, a dark brown. He was acquired from the Houghtons of Unionville through Clinton and Poppit Pitts, and when I first saw him there was some question as to whether I could cope. The Houghtons had bred him and had the dam which they found sometimes impossible to keep in a pasture enclosed with a five board fence. He was not a horse I thought of racing but I was paid a very high compliment one day by Carl and Mary Shaffer, who rode up and said "We never thought you could get along with a horse like that."

A memorable outing on Skaneatles was with the Piedmont hounds in Virginia as a result of Poppit Pitts' friendship with Paul and Eve Fout, who hosted us and our horses for a weekend. The fences were mostly stone walls, not very big. The Piedmont master said to me that he understood we had very large fences in the Elkridge-Harford country and I replied "Not many over 4 feet." The high point of the day was when Poppit introduced me to a very attractive woman rider named Jackie – yes, it was Jacqueline Kennedy Onassis. She was very pleasant and asked if I was related to Iredell Iglehart, whom she had dated while in college. It was my pleasure to give her leads over a few obstacles on Skaneatles. Those were the days!

The only time I ever thought of competing with Skaneatles was in a cross-country race that I had devised myself around Turney McKnight's farm and related properties. Among the competitors were Billy Meister, a well known timber rider, and Irv Naylor, who at the age of 55 had decided to do some serious racing, was very successful for awhile, but is now in a wheelchair on a permanent basis as a result of a fall in the Maryland Grand National. All went well, until we started down a long and very steep hill when Irv shot past me, which caused Skaneatles to bolt and run completely out of control into a field covered with multiflora rosebushes, all of 700 or 800 yards in extent. The horse jumped and dodged these bushes as fast as he could gallop. Somehow I stayed on, cleared a fence on the far side of the field, went into several large circles to regain control and finally managed to finish. Enough of that! I decided that it was time to forget about racing myself.

I was getting enough vicarious thrills from the part-ownership of a majestic, grey timberhorse named Buck Jakes. He was first discovered and trained to jump by Charlie Fenwick, who became trainer for a syndicate consisting of Andre Brewster, Peyton (Skip) Cochran, and myself known as Arcadia Stables. In addition to teaching Buck Jakes how to jump, Charlie recruited his rider, a superb, Irish horsewoman, Anne Moran, wife of Michael Moran of Unionville, Pennsylvania and mother of three children, who set the Maryland Hunt Cup course record on Jake in 1995. Returning two years later, he won again in a thrilling race. The photograph of the horse on page 132, taken in the paddock before the race, shows him in his typically regal pose, showing off for all concerned. Anne always maintained that she had little to do with his success, leaving him to figure out what to do and not interfere.

Worthless, a fine hunting mare-1975

F. N. Iglehart on Maryland Jim and J. Bosley on
Shalimar Blue-1980

Maryland Jim and Harriet after a successful
hunter pace event at Greenspring

Skaneatles-circa 1990

RACING OVER FENCES

BUCK JAKES SOARS TO SECOND MARYLAND HUNT CUP

Laurel Scott

Buck Jakes is back, and better than ever. In a near-replay of the Grand National (Md.), which he won a week earlier, Arcadia Stables' gray giant outjumped and outran a sharp Welter Weight (Michael Elmore) to notch his second Maryland Hunt Cup, April 26, with rider Anne Moran.

The 101st running of this open timber classic attracted eight stalwart entries vying for an increased purse of $50,000. They contested four firm miles and 22 stiff fences at Worthington Farms in Glyndon, Md.

Trainer Charles Fenwick Jr., a five-time winning rider of the Hunt Cup, rode Buck Jakes to a record-setting victory in Fenwick's race, the 1994 Grand National. Under Moran, Buck Jakes captured the 1994 International

Gold Cup (Va.) and the 1995 Maryland Hunt Cup (in record time). He wrapped up the fall of that year by winning his second International Gold Cup and his first Pennsylvania Hunt Cup.

Though his second Pennsylvania Hunt Cup in 1996 was a breeze, Buck Jakes was largely off his form last year, possibly due to a blood-chemistry problem. His win in the Grand National put him back in the running as a Hunt Cup favorite.

Once again, Moran and Buck Jakes faced William Meister and Club Hal Stables' Hello Hal, the lone "survivor" of last year's Hunt Cup after a virtual war of attrition. Hal was one of three Hunt Cup entries trained by William Meister, himself a three-time winner of this race.

Michael Elmore rode Welter Weight to finish a strong second in the Maryland Hunt Cup.

Meister wasn't the only trainer hedging his bets. Tom Voss had a strong double bid in Armata Stables' Welter Weight, second to Buck Jakes in the Grand National; and Bachelors' Hall's Florida Law (Joe Gillet), a three-time runner-up here.

Welter Weight, a former Gillet trainee, fell at the ninth two years ago and was pulled up after the 13th last year. Gillet piloted Florida Law in the 1994 Hunt Cup and had that ride again this year.

Another potential spoiler was Irvin Naylor's 1993 International Gold Cup winner Jamaica Bay, a Rusty Carrier trainee and 17-year-old Anne Finney's first Hunt Cup mount. Jamaica Bay was third at My Lady's Manor (Md.) on April 12.

Then there was Club Hal Stable's Red And Gray, third in the 1995 Hunt Cup and fourth in this year's Grand National. Virginian Neil Morris had the ride, his first in the Hunt Cup for trainer Meister. William Class Jr.'s skillful jumper Sarkis (Jay Meister), Billy Meister's third entry, was fifth at My Lady's Manor.

Rounding out the field was Fancy Hill Farm's Reputed Dancer, trained by Nancy Knox and ridden by another three-time Hunt Cup winner, Louis "Paddy" Neilson III. Though frustrated in two attempts at the Hunt Cup, Reputed Dancer did log a stakes victory in the St. James Hunt Cup (Ill.) last year. But he'd been off since September.

The Dynamics

It all came down to the final jump, a 3' 9½" board fence. Moran had settled Buck Jakes well off the early pace set by Jamaica Bay. She threaded her way to third by the eighth fence, and second by the 10th, where Jamaica Bay fell and Red And Gray inherited the lead.

At the 15th fence, Moran traded her methodical tracking for more aggressive tactics. Red And Gray fell here, leaving Buck Jakes to pick up the lead. His new status cued Gillet to advance

Buck Jakes looked ready to perform as Heather Bankard led him around the paddock before his second victory in the Maryland Hunt Cup.

Buck Jakes at Maryland Hunt Cup-1997

CHAPTER 24
WRONGFUL DEATH IN NORTH CAROLINA

It has always fascinated me to try a case in another state where the rules of evidence and the way to doing things may be completely different from that in Maryland. I found that out in the Hillside Hotel case and again in a fatal truck accident on Rte. 15 in North Carolina not too far from Raleigh. Another tractor trailer caused the accident and the driver of the first tractor-tractor, a resident of the Glen Burnie area of Maryland, was burned to death when the saddle tank on the driver's side ignited at the time of impact. We represented the widow, Roberta H.

Since suit would have to be filed in North Carolina, I again turned to Max Israelson for advice as to local counsel there. He recommended Charles Blanchard, who had also served on the board of the American Trial Lawyers Association. It was my job to amass the evidence with regard to our driver's earning capacity, fringe benefits under the Teamster agreement that covered him, wage trends in the industry, and so forth. I had a fascinating view of the Teamster benefits after reviewing a handbook given me by the local union office. To get a projection of wage trends in the industry, I enlisted the aid of an actuary who worked for the Social Security Administration.

In order to get a better handle on the decedent's personality, work habits, etc., I visited his widow, Roberta, at their home in Glen Burnie. There were 2 sons, one about 14 or 15, and the other about 6 or 7. Roberta was in her mid-30s, quite buxom, and attired in short-shorts. I had the impression that she did not intend to let grass grow under her feet as a widow for very long.

Suit was duly filed through Charlie Blanchard in the state court in Raleigh, and we planned for a 3 or 4 day trial there. Charlie very kindly put me up at his house on condition that I play tennis with him at the end of the day from time to time. He seemed to walk in a perpetual crouch, possibly due to an arthritic condition of the spine, but that did not slow him down on the courts where we played several nights under flood lights. It was a real workout. Our actuarial expert appeared wearing a Russian fur hat called a ushanka which he wore without inhibition on the streets of Raleigh. The trial judge permitted him to give his projections of earning capacity within the trucking industry, telling us that it was the first time such economic testimony had ever been used in a wrongful death in North Carolina. State troopers gave the basis for the liability case and it looked as if we were gathering a real head of steam for a successful conclusion.

However, as trial went on, Roberta appeared to be more and more nervous and distraught. Finally, in private conference the reason came out. She had taken up with another truck driver shortly after her husband's death and was sure that this would come out when she was cross-examined. No matter how diligently we impressed upon her that we could get an exclusionary order from the judge so that she could not be questioned about this area, she was adamant and did not want to go through the embarrassment of being questioned about her personal life. The end result was settlement for about one-half of what the case was worth because of her dread of the witness stand. It was an interesting introduction as to how things are done in North Carolina courts.

Charles Blanchard, Esq.
Raleigh, North Carolina-1988

CHAPTER 25
USES OF VIDEOTAPE

In 1984, Russell S. was employed as a guard at the Maryland House of Correction, and was on his way home when the accident occurred. He was northbound on Mt. Royal Avenue, stopped at the light in the middle lane of traffic at North Avenue with cars in the left lane waiting to make a turn onto North Avenue and cars on his right waiting to make a right turn. Russell was in the middle lane which would have led him onto the on-ramp for the Jones Falls Expressway. When the light turned green, he moved into the intersection and his car was struck violently by a delivery van traveling southbound off the JFX running a red light and making a left hand turn. The impact caused Russell to suffer brain injuries and severe facial disfigurement. He was admitted to the Shock Trauma unit at the University of Maryland hospital where a young Naval doctor treated him initially and was in charge of his case. After that, he was followed by a plastic surgeon at Johns Hopkins and left with enormous medical bills and permanent disability.

Somehow the case came to me and I filed suit against the company that owned the delivery van and the driver. Liability was so clear that defense counsel proposed that the case be tried before an arbitration panel of three, consisting of a defense attorney, a plaintiff's attorney, and a retired judge as chairman of the panel. Though the odds for a large jury award were substantial, I recommended the arbitration route to Russell in view of the time element involved as waiting for a jury trial might take years before a final resolution. The client agreed and I nominated a prominent plaintiff's attorney as one member of the panel with defense counsel nominating one of their own kind, and both sides agreed to ask Judge Reuben Oppenheimer, who had retired from the Court of Appeals, to serve as panel chairman. Both sides considered Judge Oppenheimer to be beyond reproach, and I remembered well how great a teacher he had been in the course of Conflict of Laws at Maryland Law School.

In those ancient days, the Maryland rules did not provide as they do now for the taking of depositions of expert witnesses by videotape and using them in lieu of their actual testimony in court. Rule 2-419(4). I noted a videotaped deposition of the Shock Trauma physician, who was leaving shortly for active duty as a Naval surgeon. Defense counsel moved to quash the deposition on the grounds that there was no provision in the rules for videotaping, and no provision for use of the deposition in lieu of the actual physical presence of the witness in court. The matter was heard in one day by Judge Harry Cole, who later became the first African-American judge appointed to the Court of Appeals. Judge Cole ruled in our favor asking defense counsel what possible prejudice they could show to their clients by the taking of deposition in this manner.

The case was presented before the arbitration panel in a conference room on the sixth floor of the Courthouse East where the videotaped deposition of the Shock Trauma physician was shown in addition to the taking of oral testimony. The result was an award of $400,000, which was a large sum in those days. To my knowledge, it was the first time a videotaped deposition was ever used in such a manner in Maryland.

CHAPTER 26
THE MALINGERING CLIENT

I cannot remember the name of the client or even the year that the file was opened, but I have an indelible mental image of videotape taken of her being screened in court. It was the usual rear-ender case. My client was a lady in her 50s who had been struck from behind with resulting whiplash-type injuries. As the trial date neared, I became increasingly concerned because the client's condition appeared to be getting worse and worse, and the day before the trial she appeared in my office with walking crutches which she had not used before.

Long before the trial date, I had served interrogatories upon the defendant's counsel, Wilbur D. (Woody) Preston, a distinguished senior partner in a city firm. Among the interrogatories was one asking if the defense had any still photographs or film of the plaintiff and the response had been in the affirmative, identifying the taker of the film as Interstate Detective Agency headed by Marshall M. Myer, with whom I had served in an Army Reserve unit.

I cross-examined the client very thoroughly, pointing out that the answers to interrogatories indicated that film had been taken of her when she was not aware of it. This did not dissuade her from contending that she had to have the walking crutches in order to negotiate her way to the courthouse.

I finally persuaded her to leave the walking crutches behind and to simply use a cane.

When we had closed plaintiff's case, Woody Preston asked to approach the bench and informed the trial judge that he was going to show film to the jury, and that I should have an opportunity to "voir dire" the exhibit by seeing it in advance, a routine offer. The jury was excused, a screen was set up and the film began to roll. It had been taken from a disguised delivery van with a two way window. It showed the plaintiff, a tall woman, working in her garden bent over with her legs absolutely straight, digging with a trowel in her tulip bed. She was in a pose that I could not have assumed even in prep school days. I had no basis for objecting to the film which was then shown to the jury which returned a verdict for the plaintiff and her husband in the amount of $2,000, which was about the amount of her medical bills. I think they felt sorry for her husband having to deal with the invalid.

CHAPTER 27
A CASE OF LOW "SPECIALS"

Quite the opposite result occurred in a case with only about $250 in medical bills, though the verdict was $25,000. In 1982, Andrew S. was driving to the Washington area for his defense contract work, taking the Baltimore beltway around to I-95. As he merged onto 95, a tractor-trailer was moving in and out of traffic, rapidly changing lanes and then colliding with his vehicle from the rear, pushing it laterally across three lanes of highway and smashing it up against a guardrail. Other than the damage to his vehicle, Andrew's injuries consisted of a sore knee that had banged against the stirring column and a bump on his head from hitting the roof of the car.

The happening of the accident, particularly seeing the tractor-trailer bearing down on him, had had an extremely traumatic effect. Andrew began having sensations of losing his eyesight and he began making the medical rounds from ophthalmologist to neurologist to orthopedist, each of whom readily referred him on to the next specialist because his complaints seemed rather bizarre. The last straw was when the neurologist recommended a psychiatrist whom he refused to consult.

All this was laid out before the jury on a typical Baltimore winter day with a pending snowstorm in the offing. In addition to the medical bills and very brief medical testimony, Andrew's son testified to working with his father several days after the accident, helping him put down insulation in the attic of his house where he seemed to be extremely agitated and unable to find his way back down the ladder from the attic. That concluded the plaintiff's case and the court adjourned for the day.

A wet snow descended during the night and the next day the County schools were closed which was the automatic signal that the jurors did not have to come in. Defense counsel was quite upset because he had air tickets for Jamaica with his family for the following day, and I proposed that the jury commissioner poll the jurors on the case to see which ones would be willing to hazard the drive in to the courthouse. We readily agreed to this and the result was 7 interested jurors appeared, who in due course returned a verdict for $25,000 which had no relationship to the amount of "specials" in the case. They had empathized completely with Andrew's terror at being run down by the tractor-trailer.

A few months later at a Bar Association party, Judge Cicone, the administrative judge, came up to me and growled "Iglehart, you're gonna ruin our system around here by bringing these kind of cases to trial" – a typical comment for a former insurance adjuster.

CHAPTER 28
THE ALCOHOLIC CLIENT

A childhood friend who came back to haunt me in the 1970s and 1980s was Robert O., nicknamed "Bucky," a dedicated alcoholic. I tried to help him by managing his finances and keeping him out of jail, but it was a daunting task. In 1966, Maryland National Bank was appointed his mother's guardian. Under a little known provision of the Maryland Equity Code, the bank had been authorized to support Bucky out of the guardianship as one who had been maintained and supported in part by his mother prior to the creation of the guardianship. I made arrangements with the bank's trust officer, George Elder, to send me the monthly stipend so that I could take care of his rent and give him a small amount for food.

Bucky's bouts with the bottle were constant despite two stays at Hidden Brook, a rehabilitation place for alcoholics in Harford County. To supplement the funds coming to him out of his mother's guardianship, Bucky started stealing silver from friends and acquaintances' houses at a time when the silver market was very high. One such theft occurred in west Towson and Bucky meandered down the street passing the District Court office where Judge Hinkel was seated in chambers looking out his window and saw Bucky staggering along with silver spoons and forks spilling from his pockets.

In 1984, his attraction for silver caused him to steal from acquaintances' homes in the Berryville, Virginia area where he was finally arrested, charged and locked up in the Luray jail. Misperceiving him as a good risk to become a "trusty", the warden appointed him to the job of cutting lawns outside the jail, and with less than 3 weeks to serve on his sentence, he eloped, the elopement lasting several years. I notified the trust officer that Bucky was a fugitive from justice and that it would be appropriate to hold up his monthly checks until he surrendered to the authorities, as otherwise the trust company might become implicated in the escape.

For a period of several years, Bucky survived by his wits, borrowing money and a place to sleep through local AA organizations from Atlantic City, New Jersey to Saratoga, New York. After many tries, I finally persuaded Bucky to board a plane in Albany, New York and fly to Baltimore where I met him and we boarded a plane for Staunton, Virginia where I rented a car and I drove him to Luray to surrender himself at the jail. The warden was somewhat surprised, but the local prosecuting attorney said to take him away, he never wanted to see him again and have to bother with the paperwork that he had caused.

An aunt residing in New York state died, and Bucky inherited approximately $100,000 outright, which sum I forced him to invest in an annuity, practically at gunpoint, with the provision that he receive a monthly payment for life and a certain fixed sum would go to his two daughters upon his death for a period of years. I arranged for him to live in an apartment near the Johns Hopkins campus where I paid the rent and worked out a food allowance for him. I filed a Petition in his mother's guardianship to give Maryland National Bank discretion and authority to pay the debts that he had accumulated during the long period of his elopement from the Luray jail, and a modest amount for counsel fee.

Somehow Bucky survived for a few more years and eventually died from a heart attack in 1993. Things didn't seem to be quite the same without him around.

CHAPTER 29
CECE'S CASE

Though I had given several negative opinions to prospective clients who felt that they had claims of medical malpractice against one physician or another, I had only one case where we actually filed suit. CeCe, short for Cecilia, was a registered nurse, and her husband, Stephen, who was a third year medical student, elected to have thoracic surgery performed at St. Agnes Hospital by a leading thoracic surgeon to repair the valve that keeps food from being aspirated into the lungs. He died in the hospital in 1972. The case was referred to me by R. Edwin Brown in Rockville, with whom I had tried the ladder case many years before, and he had a young associate named Dennis Ettlin, who had roomed with Stephen at the University of Maryland College Park.

After performing the surgery, the surgeon left the next day on a vacation trip to the Bahamas, leaving no senior person in charge of Stephen's case. He developed an infection which ultimately resulted in renal failure and death, the orders for antibiotics always seeming to be about 24 hours late in being implemented.

Other than the theory of abandonment, the only thing we had to go on was what the Physicians Desk Reference book (PDR) said about the various antibiotics that had eventually been given to Stephen. CeCe had a daughter born post-humously and this made her economic situation even more difficult than it would if Stephen had survived. I found her a charming person to deal with and became aware of the deep antipathy between the nursing profession and the medical doctors, the "M-Deities." At one point in the case preparation, she arranged a session in the home of a fellow nurse in the Glen Burnie area on a Saturday where three young nurses and CeCe went through Stephen's chart with me for hours on end, pointing out why his care was inadequate as the infection progressed.

Then one day CeCe came to see me very distressed and embarrassed. She told me that her in-laws, who lived in New York City, had contacted Melvin Belli at his office in San Francisco and had asked him to enter the case as co-counsel with me. In due course, Belli's appearance was entered in the case through a so-called associate, who was a member of the Maryland Bar with offices in Rockville. Defense counsel taunted me asking if I really believed that Belli would appear at trial. They were willing to bet that he would not. I was going to San Francisco to attend an American Trial Lawyers Convention and made an arrangement to meet "the great man" at his offices there to go over certain aspects of the case. When the day of the meeting in San Francisco arrived, I was, frankly, impressed with Belli's questions about the case. The only thing that bothered me was that we broke off for lunch about mid-way through the case review, which had already taken several hours, and repaired to a seafood restaurant where Melvin Belli consumed three martinis and a glass of wine before returning to the office for further case review.

Eventually, we had a trial date and a negotiating session was scheduled with defense counsel consisting of two renowned defense attorneys in the medical malpractice field. They made an offer in the six figure range and pressed me pretty hard with the usual comments about the train leaving the station and so forth. I made an appointment with CeCe for the following day to review the offer and where we stood in the case. When I asked her if she was mentally and emotionally prepared for the possibility of a defendant's verdict, rating our chances at about 50/50, her eyes welled up with tears and she confessed that she was not prepared for such an eventuality. It was then that we both decided to settle for the figure offered.

Melvin Belli had not contributed anything to producing the offer made and he was not consulted, though it was indicated to me that he expected to split the fee on a 50/50 basis. The settlement checks only had my name on them as CeCe's attorney. I decided the honorable thing to do was to negotiate the checks, deducting the amount of the contingent fee and placing that sum in a special escrow account with an interpleader filed in court asking whatever judge got the matter to make the decision as to how the fee should be split. The matter was finally heard one day by Judge Joseph Caplan, the administrative judge of the Circuit Court for Baltimore City. He urged a compromise, but the forwarding attorney, R. Edwin Brown, refused any compromise and Caplan said he was reluctantly ruling against us.

I had learned quite a bit of medicine in the course of preparing the case, and also about Melvin Belli. In spite of all that, CeCe and I remain good friends and I consider her a client. Recently, Harriet and I attended her daughter's wedding.

CHAPTER 30
ESTATES

The longer one is in the practice of law, the more one will be involved in clients' estates whether one has done their Wills or not. What follows are three accounts to illustrate that one can never take things for granted in matters of estate law.

Perpetuities

In 1984, my cousin, George, died suddenly while seated quietly in his chiropractor's office reading a magazine. George was quite well-to-do, having far more in the way of worldly assets than anyone on our side of the family but one would never know it from his lifestyle. He was divorced and lived in an early 19th century farmhouse on the farm that he owned on Dover Road where he raised cattle. The raising of cattle was somewhat haphazard as he had any number of bulls running freely in the herd. A more successful aspect of his farming operation was the raising of chickens and eggs on a mass production basis. That did not make some neighbors very happy. Though a staunch Republican, George was host when Khrushchev himself came to see this mass production that rivaled Mr. Perdue.

George asked me to do his Will and I accompanied him to meetings at Mercantile-Safe Deposit & Trust Co. George normally attired in his farm clothes and wearing muddy boots, presented quite a sight in the formal quarters of the bank. After generous bequests to the charities that he had contributed substantially to over the years, such as the Visiting Nurse Association and Reading for the Blind, he left his residuary estate to his daughter and two sons in trust for life with the remainder to their issue. Since the bequest in trust terminated at the death of each of the three children, the life tenants, I considered them as measuring lives and that there was no need for a special clause invoking the rule against perpetuities stating who were the measuring lives and that any trust would terminate within 21 years of the last death. The officials at the Trust Department of the bank thought otherwise and sought a court ruling as to whether or not the trusts were valid. To my consternation, the Court of Appeals ultimately ruled that the rule against perpetuities rendered the trusts invalid, complete distribution then going to the three children.

It took several years before this decision was rendered and my work as Personal Representative went on. After disposing of the cattle herd, I then tackled the job of doing something to make the place more marketable, re-fencing the entire 200 acres, in consultation with head of the paneling committee of the local hunt club, reconstructing the porch in line with a design appropriate to the early 19th century, rebuilding the interior where joists had given way, painting, etc. The end result was a transformed property which was ultimately sold to the former headmaster of Gilman School and his wife for the amount of its appraisal and the cost of repairs and improvements. Their son raises Angus cattle and they breed both flat and steeplechase horses, considered by all the neighbors as great additions to the community.

Not long after the Court of Appeals decision came down, George's youngest son, Steve, who lived in Colorado and ran a river-rafting company, died of a heart attack following a severe attack of asthma. His Will left everything to various environmental groups which would not have received anything of significance had there been no rule against perpetuities. George's daughter, Edie, is now married and living in Flagstaff, Arizona. His son, Jeffrey, lives near his mother in Staunton, Virginia and has a commercial pilot's license, presumably his inheritance has gone into the aviation business.

I still do not fully understand the Court of Appeals ruling, but I never did fully understand the rule against perpetuities except that it is better to have a special clause in any Will where it might otherwise create a problem.

The Value of Tangible Items

I had done another Will for a delightful, elderly lady client named Peggy, in her late

80s, who lived on a small farm property not too far from George's place. She had two daughters separated in ages by many years, one a widow, the other married and living near Philadelphia. Peggy named me and her broker, Frank Galletti, as Co-Personal Representatives in her Will, saying that she knew that her two daughters would not get along and there would only be delay and serious problems in settling her estate if they were named instead. Peggy moved to Oxford, Pennsylvania to a retirement home where she was quite happily situated not too far from her two daughters and grandchildren. So her domicile became Chester County, Pennsylvania where her Will was eventually probated upon her death in 1995. Other than charitable bequests, the Will left everything in equal shares to the two daughters, including tangible items consisting mostly of her furnishings in her apartment at the retirement home which were to be divided up, the dividing being the responsibility of Frank and myself.

We had all the tangible items appraised and then it was agreed that the older daughter, Anna, and Meg, the younger, would pick from the list on a special date. The one to make the first selection was determined by a flip of the coin, the rest of the selections being made on a rotation basis. On the day for the division, Frank had the forethought to hire a video cameraman to photograph all items in the apartment, naming them as they were in the appraisal list. All went smoothly, to such an extent that the younger daughter, Meg, who was of a religious bent, had the four of us join hands in a circle while she gave prayers of thanks for the peaceful division of her mother's items.

Within days, phone calls came from Meg, somewhat hysterical, claiming that she had been cheated, that the rotation system was unfair, and that the whole division of tangible items had to be re-done. Fortunately, Frank and I had retained the services of Richard Jones, Esq., a partner in the firm of Prickett, Jones, et al. located in Kennett Square, Pennsylvania, and we ultimately had not one, but two, full scale evidentiary hearings before a probate judge in Chester County. His decision endorsed our method of division and the only thing was to dispose of items that nobody wanted. Meg suggested a local church and we said fine, though within a matter of days, she complained that the church had been cheated and had not received enough, there were items never accounted for, etc. etc. I suggested to Frank, and he agreed, that we would solve the problem by making gifts of $250 each to the church out of our commissions. That seemed to settle matters as we have not heard anymore about it over the last several years.

Catch 22

R. Edwin Brown and his law partner, Rex L. Sturm, had an unusual matter involving an estate in Montgomery County. The problem was making an effective claim against the estate for a substantial sum of money. Ed Brown had a client named William Parrico, who owned a large dairy farm which was in the path of development. Parrico asked Brown to assist him in the sale of the farm and made him his agent. There was a written undertaking that Brown and Sturm would receive 8% commissions on a contract that he had negotiated for him. This amounted to over $800,000. When Parrico died in 1986, Ed Brown wrote his Personal Representative, one William Moore, sending him a copy of the agency agreement and an accounting of sales on which the 8% commissions had been taken. He continued to take commissions on additional sales, remitting the balance to Moore, who finally, more than six months after the date of death, advised Brown that he would not honor the agency arrangement as Brown had not made a formal claim against the estate.

Brown was not going to give up his $800,000 in commissions without a fight and suit was filed in Federal Court in Baltimore, the case being assigned to Judge Black, who ruled on a Motion for Summary Judgment in Moore's favor. That was followed by an appeal to the Fourth Circuit Court of Appeals which reversed and sent the case back to permit the filing of Brown's original transmittal letter to Moore to see whether it met the requirements of the Maryland Probate Code as a claim against the estate.

The case was then reassigned to Judge Nickerson, who again granted a Motion for Summary Judgment in favor of the estate with another appeal to the Fourth Circuit where a new panel of three judges affirmed Judge Nickerson. I asked for a rehearing *en banc* but only got 3 out of 11 votes of the judges on the Fourth Circuit for a rehearing.

Ed Brown wanted to go to the Supreme Court but I demurred, taking the position that I felt that I had done all I could, and that it was not a case where certiorari would be granted. We would have won if Brown's original transmittal letter to Moore had simply stated "I am hereby making a claim against the estate in accordance with Section such & such of the Maryland Probate Code." - a seemingly artificial requirement, but nevertheless essential if one is to avoid a true catch 22 situation.

CHAPTER 31
TEENAGE DRIVERS

Dawn's case was referred to me by John W. Hessian III, with whom J. Michael McLaughlin and I were sharing office space in the building known as the Nottingham Building located at 102 W. Pennsylvania Avenue in Towson. We severed our physical association with Hessian when it was determined that he was embezzling funds from various estates that he was personal representative of – a tragic situation that led to his disbarment.

Dawn was a high school senior out on a date with her steady boyfriend on a Saturday night. After stopping at a drive-in for Cokes and hotdogs in the Jarrettsville area, then proceeding south on Rt. 152, her date, who was driving, asked her to hold the wheel while he unwrapped his hotdog. The direct result of this imprudent maneuver was their vehicle crossing the center line, hitting another one northbound head-on, killing the driver of that vehicle and causing serious injuries to both of them. Dawn suffered a closed head injury without skull fracture, but the brain damage was just as serious, impairing her ability to speak, write, and ambulate.

The estate of the deceased driver settled with Dawn's boyfriend for his policy limits, and they executed a general release so there was still a possibility of collecting from her boyfriend's insurance carrier.

I took the boyfriend's deposition to establish how the accident occurred with his admission of surrendering the steering wheel to Dawn at precisely the wrong time and place.

Dawn had been transferred from a local Harford County hospital to a rehabilitation center in Bryn Mawr, Pennsylvania where her rehabilitation from her serious brain injury went on for more than a year. I went up several times with her parents to meet with the different therapists and review her painstaking progress. Dramatic evidence of improvement was shown in samples of handwriting, the first one showing a huge scrawl written with letters taking up most of the page of the notepaper, later reducing in size to the point that they were legible and normal in appearance. Armed with her boyfriend's deposition and a transcript of all the work that had been done at the Bryn Mawr rehabilitation center, I submitted a demand for policy limits of $100,000 which was accepted after some understandable delay on defense counsel's part.

I have often wondered how Dawn made out in later life. Her case taught me a great deal about the effects of closed head injuries.

CHAPTER 32
HIGHER AUTHORITY

For us in Maryland, the Fourth Circuit Court of Appeals with headquarters in Richmond, VA is our place of higher authority since getting to the Supreme Court is so difficult. I have had the experience of going to the Fourth Circuit four times starting with the flammable fabrics case and each time I felt as if I was truly dealing with higher authority. The court is situated in a square in Richmond, adorned with statues of Robert E. Lee and other Confederates. A convenient place to stay nearby is the Commonwealth Park Hotel where they only have suites, not rooms. When you finish making your argument before a panel of three judges, they descend from the bench and come to shake hands with counsel on both sides, a very pleasant practice.

The second time I argued Ed Brown's case before the Court in 1990, Judge Chapman said to me when he came down to shake hands: "Three strikes and you're out." My response was "Your Honor, I've only had two strikes so far." In spite of ultimately losing, it was and is a pleasant experience to recall.

In conclusion, it will appear that in spite of being only an "occasional attorney" with other interests than the law, the practice of the profession can involve one in almost every conceivable situation that one's fellow humans can create - hardly a boring life. In the long run, as imperfect as it is, the growth of the law may be the only thing to save our planet from incineration.

CHAPTER 33
BOATS

Besides involvement in the horse world, from the age of 11 or 12 I became enamored with boats. My parents had started renting a house in Northeast Harbor, Maine in the late 1930s, previously having gone to Saranac Lake for the summer, and they enrolled me in a sailing class with the Fleet. The boat of choice was a 15' unsinkable sloop called a Bullseye. The second year, we chartered a gaff-rigged, Lawley A boat with running back stays. You learned more sailing with the A boat, but their age was such that when you had any degree of wind to apply pressure to the mast, the seams below began to open up requiring a good deal of bailing.

After several years of A boats, at the age of 16, I was asked to race an international for the Edison family from Philadelphia during the month of August. I formed a crew of three other 16 year olds: Eddie Brennan, Lenny Marshall, and a third whose name I cannot remember. We were reasonably successful finishing in the middle of the Fleet for the series, the only mishap being a blown-out spinnaker on one occasion. That was the summer of 1941. World War II intervened and the following summer I was loading freight cars at the Crown Cork & Seal plant in east Baltimore. This was supposedly part of the war effort, though the B series of gasoline rationing coupons enabled me to take a Saturday night date to the movies or the

162

Summit nightclub to dance to Louis Prima's band.

It was some years after the war when I chartered a boat from the Hinckley Company in Southwest Harbor, Maine, a Pilot 35 sloop-rigged with a roller furling jib which made it easy for a crew of two to sail. It wasn't until 1975 that the thought of ownership carried me away. An idle conversation with Bob Hinckley, son of Henry Hinckley, the founder of the company, revealed that a Hinckley 41 owned by someone named Bud Diesinger of Philadelphia, was for sale. The 41 was just that overall in length, slept six in a squeeze, had a full 6' keel, and was very stable, but not very fast. The negotiated price was $51,000. The best investment I ever made.

Two sons applauded the move, Tom, then working in the Boston area, and John, a student at Tufts, both of whom suggested finding some place to keep the boat near to the Boston area. Our eldest son, Frank, was then in Boulder, Colorado after his graduation from the university. I talked to Bob Hinckley, who strongly recommended someone named Raz Parker, who had a yard on the south side of Buzzard's Bay about five miles from the Cape Cod canal. This was the beginning of a strong friendship with a unique individual, an old salt, who had been in the Merchant Marine in World War II. Raz was the son of an Episcopal minister who was a Navy chaplain and Raz was born in American Samoa. He knew boats and was a great raconteur. At the end of the summer of

1975, I moved the boat to Parkers Boat Yard after stops in Narangansett Bay. For the big run south from Maine to the Cape Cod area, the crew consisted of myself, son John, Art Gompf and Rip Poole, who at the time were building a fence line around a pasture field on Ivy Hill property at home. It soon became clear from a number of trips, that Tom and John had inherited their mother's tendency to become violently seasick upon any motion of a boat. This rendered them basically incapable for offshore sailing, though they tried valiantly to overcome the handicap. I was never able to get Frank on board. Hallie had the same problem as we found from a sail in the Caribbean, and before that, Laney had shown similar symptoms of *mal de mer* off of Cape Breton Island.

Every odd year was the Marblehead to Halifax race, and in 1977 it seemed like the thing to do. In his enthusiasm, Tom forgot his seaworthy problem and joined the race crew consisting of Art, Rip, Jack Voss, and Bruce Parker, Raz's son. I had renamed the Diesinger boat "Shenandoah" in honor of my great-great-Confederate uncle, Capt. Iredell Waddell of post-Civil War fame. It was the best race she was ever in. At the start, I estimated the distance to the Committee boat by timing the gun from the appearance of the smoke until the report reached our ears. Assuming a sound speed of 1,100 feet per second and converting that factor to the speed needed to cross the line from the time the Genoa was unfurled, enabled us to cross the line right on the money. It was a 360 mile distance to Halifax, and I decided to cut the corner and go in close to Cape Sable and Brazil Rock rather than standing way off shore to avoid the Fundy tide. According to the Eldridges Tide Catalog, the time of our arrival off Cape Sable would be at the moon's apogee – the furthest from the earth when the Fundy tide would have the least effect. Many boats stayed up to 30 miles offshore passing Cape Sable, but we were in very close and finished in the middle of the class ahead of us, and ahead of most of the boats in our class - not bad for a bunch of beginners.

The Royal Halifax Yacht Club provided a safe berth for Shenandoah, and I enlisted Art, Rip, and Bob Constable as crew to take her on to Cape Breton Island later in the summer. For me, the Bras d'Or Lakes of Cape Breton was the Ultimate Thule of sailing, and I spent many a happy time there on Shenandoah and other craft. The first winter, I left the boat at Henry Fuller's yard in Baddeck with an eye on sailing to Newfoundland the following summer. For the run to Newfoundland, I picked a select crew: Art, Rip, and Raz. Raz was to get off at the French island of St. Pierre where he would be replaced by his son, Bruce. The problem with that plan was that Air Canada went on strike and Raz had to stay with us for the entire trip to the Newfoundland south shore, St. Pierre, and the return to Southwest Harbor, Maine. We cast off from a small fishing port on the east side of Cape Breton for the 90 mile run to a place called White Bear Bay inside the Ramea Islands where there was a radio direction station, the only one on the south coast of Newfoundland. We figured that if we left around mid-afternoon, we would have all of the following day to find our way into White Bear Bay.

The trip went faster than expected as a strong front moved in, driving us at breakneck speed on a reach with a long line rigged as a preventer to keep the mainsail from jibing. The following seas were threatening to swamp the cockpit as racing clouds flew across a pale moon. An encounter with lights ahead that appeared to be those of a super-tanker caused us great anxiety as we were unable to maneuver due to the strength of the wind. To our amazement, the great craft began turning away from our headlong course and we passed her safely.

As the night wore on, fatigue caused me to begin to hallucinate. I swore I could see an Indian with a full headdress climbing over the stern from time to time. Dawn showed a reddish-brown coastline consisting of bluffs that looked very high. The Ramea signal was pretty strong and our dead reckoning had put us where we thought we should be. As we sailed past the Ramea Islands, our problem was finding the entrance to White Bear Bay. All we could see was a solid line of bluffs 800-900 feet high. Finally, we saw the entrance which had been hidden due to the fact that we were coming at it at an oblique angle which screened the opening. White Bear Bay was a natural fjord and we had to proceed up it almost five miles before we could find any holding ground. By nightfall, the temperature was just above freezing and the stars formed the most luminous canopy I had ever seen. The entire south coast of Newfoundland is devoid of human habitation, the provincial government having moved people away because of the lack of resources. The only fellow humans that we encountered was the following morning when a small fishing boat chugged up to hail us and we were presented with a large codfish. The crew of the fishing boat consisted of Canadians from Toronto, who were vacationing on the Ramea Islands. I guess they wanted to get away from it all. We left fairly early that morning to make the run to St. Pierre where we looked forward to encountering civilization again with a French accent. The run down consisting of two long reaches was uneventful, and we were gratified to enter a busy harbor with a large shed near the entrance and a sign with Douane on it. We cleared Customs at St. Pierre and rented a room at a nearby hotel where the four of us took turns showering and shaving. After a very civilized meal, we decided to explore the nightlife of St. Pierre by walking up to a building on the top of a hill overlooking the harbor that had a neon star blinking on and off - "L'Etoile" where the patrons were half local inhabitants and half vacationing Newfoundlanders. The music was mostly fast waltzes. Though he did not speak a word of French, Raz decided to get us partners from among the ladies for a dance or two. Protocol decreed that only one dance was allowed per partner as otherwise it would appear something more serious was going on. The next day, we rented motorbikes and toured the island. On the second day, it was time to reprovision for the long run back to Southwest Harbor, Maine. For ice, we were guided to a fish packing plant where we filled plastic bags with crushed ice which provided excellent refrigeration in the locker with a blanket folded on top. A 38' sloop tied up next to us with four young Frenchman who had sailed from Brittany to Spitzbergen, and endured a knockdown off the Newfoundland east coast, a voyage that made ours pale into insignificance. With them we observed a classic phenomenon. After many long days and nights at sea, they seemed to be tied to their boat by an invisible umbilical cord and did not spend any leisure time ashore. The first night out from St. Pierre we were treated to Northern Lights – we hoped a good omen. Shifting veils of darkness and silverly light reaching halfway from the horizon to the zenith over our heads – an extraordinary display.

The following day, static on the radio indicated bad weather approaching from ahead. The sky began to turn a milky yellow color and before long we were into a real storm with waves 15-20' high. We had a reefed main and storm jib but still were losing the control needed to traverse the waves rather than pitching straight down into them. We tried the storm jib alone, then the reefed main by itself, but nothing gave us the kind of control we wanted. Plunging into the waves with resounding crashes, caused Raz to say "I hope Henry didn't cut any corners when he built this one," referring to Henry Hinckley, the proprietor of the boat building company. In fact, Shenandoah had a fiberglass bow almost three inches in thickness and was very well built. Somehow in the chaos of our passage, Art was able to bake a loaf of beer bread which sustained us through the day as we took turns on the tiller negotiating the fearful wave crests.

Finally, after sundown, the storm began to abate and by midnight things were positively peaceful. We had no way of knowing how much the leeway factor resulting from the storm might have put us off our course, and I began to have an eerie feeling like a prickling on my scalp. Rip was with me on watch and I said "Lets check the depth finder." Sure enough it was going from 90 to 80 to 60 feet, and just then we could hear a foghorn blowing in a sequence that put us within several miles of the Cape Breton shore. It was time to tack over and get out of there, which we did, running through the following morning off of Sable Island - the infamous graveyard of ships. We checked our DR with radio direction fixes and Art got the Halifax Coast Guard to give us a longitudinal fix when we were approximately 40 miles off the harbor. Late on the fourth night, Rip and I were again on watch and were astonished to see a glowing form in the shape of a torpedo-like projectile racing towards the hull and passing underneath. This was repeated time after time and we could only assume that it was either dolphins or pilot whales having a bit of a game with us. The water was full of phosphorescence. Our crude navigation worked and in due course we made Mt. Desert Rock, then the Duck Islands, Baker, Cranberry and Sutton Islands, smelling the delightful aroma of pinewood smoke from fireplaces. It was an easy run in then to Southwest Harbor where we picked up a Hinckley Company buoy and turned in about 3:00 a.m. The entire 600 mile trip had been made without GPS or Loran, which we later deemed to be essential for serious cruising in later years.

The problem with recollections is that you lose a year or two here or there unless you have a diary or a carefully kept log. I think it was two years before that Tom, John, Bob Constable and I took the boat up the St. John's River and back, hazarding the Reversing Falls and its 15 minute window of opportunity for passing at the time of slack tide – all without mishap. It was a revelation to traverse 50 miles of the river inland as far as Grand Lake and back.

After the 1977 Halifax race and trip to Newfoundland, we decided to take a shot at the Annapolis to Newport race in 1980, and took the boat down the coast around Cape May and up Delaware Bay blithely assuming it would be an easy run even at night, not allowing for the confusion of lights on shore and churning tugboats putting their spotlights on us. Art and Rip were the crew with a friend of theirs, and I was sound asleep in my bunk when a resounding crash and hollow bell like sound propelled me up into the cockpit to find that we had run into a large oil drum helping to support dredge lines at the mouth of the Delaware and Chesapeake Canal, all without major damage to the boat.

The Annapolis to Newport race was a complete fiasco. Dead calm at the start with anchors down waiting for some air and later down the Bay, a mighty struggle with thousands of flies that came onboard while we hoped and prayed for a thunder storm. Drifting backward without wind off of Cape Henry for a period of 6 or 7 hours, finally put the quietus on our hopes and we abandoned the race, motoring into Cape May to refuel with perhaps only vapors to operate the engine as we entered the harbor. A stop on the East River and traversing Long Island Sound provided some interest to the aborted race. 1981 was another year for a try at Halifax, but the moon was not in the apogee and we had to stay out from Cape Sable, not finishing nearly as well as in 1977.

By 1982, the boat was pretty well "shook down" and able-bodied sailors were available for crew to do the Newport to

Bermuda race. Those who signed on were Art and Rip, Henry Pitts, Chris Westerlund, David Westerlund, GB Gordon, and Paul Swenson, CEO of the Moran Towing Co., all quartered on a boat big enough for four on an extended overnight. What ensued was the worst sailing trip ever for most of us: from the edge of the Gulf Stream for 72 hours, a series of line squalls coming out of inky-black skies accompanied by icy downblasts at several times flattening the boat to the point where the spreaders were in the water. Somehow we managed to sail the Rhumb line and took our turns off watch trying to sleep on sail bags piled up in the cabin. Our only food for most of the trip was a Smithfield ham that GB Gordon had bought at Eddie's Supermarket in Baltimore and brought with him. We were so spaced out from fatigue that as we approached Bermuda, Art, our navigator, and I argued endlessly whether we should follow the disrupted Loran signals or switch over to a radio direction finder, losing hours sailing back and forth at right angles to the Rhumb line until we finally decided to go in with the radio signals in the early morning hours of the fifth day. The fact that we were second to last in the entire fleet didn't bother us. We had survived!

We decided to profit somehow from this terrible trip and a commitment was made that Chris Westerlund would stay with the boat in Bermuda and that Art, Rip, and I would rejoin him in November after the hurricane season for a run through to the islands of the Caribbean, which turned out to be as memorable and pleasant a trip as ours to Bermuda had been atrocious.

Chris was happy with the arrangement as he was seeking to avoid Internal Revenue at home, which was pursuing him for unreported income from his scalloping operation in Nantucket. He survived on a modest monetary allowance and Rip, Art, and I rejoined him shortly after Thanksgiving. Shenandoah was now equipped with Loran which packed in and failed completely a day out of Bermuda on the run south. Fortunately, Art had his sextant and celestial navigation tables with him and set to work with star sights and moon shots at night while I attempted noon sights in the daytime. We averaged the results as we proceeded and had some help from a Russian freighter en route to Cuba which gave us our position and wished us a good trip in heavily accented English.

Chris had purchased an Aries steering vane designed by an eccentric investor in Bristol, England which was connected to the tiller with a yoke and chain arrangement, and when we picked up the tradewind Aries did most of the sailing while we were on a broad reach with big following seas. Six days and nights put us on the north side of St. Thomas and rather than run in at nighttime, we hove to and waited for the morning to see our way in. From St. Thomas we moved on to Tortola and then on to St. Maarten where we left the boat with Chris in charge for the beginning of a Caribbean idyll that lasted 2 ½ years with countless airfares to St. Maarten, Martinique, and Grenada – an easy life to adjust to.

Hallie succumbed to the family problem on a run from St. Maarten to St. Barts. Even Harriet tried one passage, but soon succumbed after we came out from under the lee of St. Vincent to big ocean swells.

The best run in the islands that we experienced was from St. Barts to Nevis past St. Kitts on a broad reach down and tight reach coming back. Something to remember for a long time. Grenada was an interesting trip. We got there about one month after what they call the "Intervention" – walls of the houses were spray painted with slogans such as "God Bless the 82nd Airborne" and similar thanks for assistance from the USA. We were on a high hill overlooking a soccer field on their Labor Day when we heard the sound of insistent drumming coming from perhaps a mile away. A phalanx of red-shirted members of the Transport Workers Union came into view, marching 10 abreast to the stadium. We decided to slip down behind the stadium to hear the revolutionary harangues that would ensue, but all we heard were gospel readings and psalms. After two and a half years, it came time to call an end to our visits to paradise. Chris Westerlund wanted to relocate to Nantucket, and it seemed time to gain some control over the sailing budget.

The trip north was from St. Thomas past Puerto Rico with a stop at Puerto Plata in the Dominican Republic, the Bahamas, and then Ft. Lauderdale. The only interesting event on the trip was a Coast Guard vessel that shadowed us for many miles and then radioed us to heave-to to prepare for boarding. We told them it would take half an hour to get the spinnaker and other sails down. Their response was to prepare for boarding regardless. A launch appeared with 6 Coast Guardsman armed with M-16s and a Bosun, who managed to fall overboard in trying to transfer from the launch to the cockpit of Shenandoah. All that we could see of him was the knuckles of his hands holding on to the gunwale for dear life. This broke the ice and we passed inspection. In the run north from Ft. Lauderdale in the Gulf Stream we made close to 200 miles in a 24 hour period, eventually pulling in near Morehead City.

In due course, a few months later Shenandoah was back in Maine tied up on the dock at Bass Harbor Marina. I was having a cup of coffee early in the morning when a figure came running down the gangplank and asked me if by any chance the boat was for sale. I hemmed and hawed and said that I hadn't thought about it, having "family" sailing plans for the end of the summer. I was talking to a Hinckley Company salesman who had clients in the form of a doctor from Texas and his wife who wanted above all things to acquire a Hinckley 41, since only a dozen or so had been built. I felt it was time to move on and make a deal as the boat wasn't getting any younger, nor was I, and the matter was settled for $75,000 – an amazing increase due the inflation in boat values at the time. A happy ending to 10 years of sailing on a very seaworthy boat.

I was not to remain boatless for long, however, as Bob Hinckley's people knew how to bait a trap the right way. Rather than the direct approach, I was asked if I could help crew a new yawl-rigged 42 down to Annapolis from the Stamford, Connecticut area. The company had one man on the boat, an experienced young sailor named Pablo McGrail. Including myself, I said I would provide three additional crew members and signed up Art and Rip for the run south. It was such a fast trip that I was hooked. The hook was placed more securely the following year when I was invited to race a new 42, as yet unsold, in an around-the-islands event followed by a sunflower raft gathering on Somes Sound. The salesman assigned to me was Hank Halsted, who really knew his sales psychology. In due course, papers were signed to have a new sloop-rigged 42 built. Shenandoah II extended my sailing career by 9 years with old and new crewmembers who were happy to come on board for more Halifax races, trips to Newfoundland, and even another Bermuda race with the benefit of radar, GPS, and Loran.

For that year's Bermuda race, we had as crew Art and Rip, Bruce Parker, Chris

Westerlund and his brother David, and Bam LaFarge from Nantucket, a grandson of Oliver LaFarge, and Annie Lewandowski, once briefly a cook on a seagoing tug who had crewed for me many times. In spite of having such an excellent crew, we were quite unsuccessful in the race, but better able to enjoy Bermuda when we got there than the first time. The problem with Bermuda racing was that you had to bring the boat back and usually your race crew all jumped ship. For the return voyage that year, I had my nephew, Jay Howard, Rip, Annie, and a girl who worked for Hinckley as a rigger but who seemed to think that we were supposed to wait on her in terms of washing, cooking, and so forth. We started somewhat late in the day after several days in Bermuda and we were fortunate to be behind the lead boat returning, which ran into fearsome weather causing demasting, broken rudders, and other problems which we could hear about over the single sideband radio.

Another memorable adventure with the new boat was in the year 1994 when we decided to assay the St. John's River with a crew consisting of Art, Rip, Raz, Stanley Dorman, Don Greenawalt, and myself. As we approached the Reversing Falls just beyond St. John's Harbor, I congratulated myself on my assumed perfect timing making the approach run. According to my calculations, we were going to be exactly there at slack tide without the necessity of having to tie-up at a freighter pier en route. We told the St.

John's Coast Guard on the radio that were going to make the run through the Falls and did not pay attention to the response, which was something to the effect that we were a bit late. We were in fact an hour late, not having reset our watches for Atlantic time. The water seemed to be running very fast through the narrow gorge, but the boat made it to a point near the paper mill where all forward motion ceased. With the engine maxed out, it was clear that were losing the battle against the current and began to debate whether to try to move backwards with it or turn and run. Just then, two speeding boats came into view, one a Royal Mounted police boat and the other belonging to the Coast Guard. They were involved in an experiment to throw dummies overboard and film what happened to them in the swirling current. We waved frantically to them and fortunately got a tow from both boats lined up in tandem ahead of us. It was a close call. That evening back at the local yachtclub, the 6 o'clock tv news in the bar showed the entire episode as the video cameraman concentrated on our rescue operation. We were referred to as "American tourists" not as sailors. For days afterwards, in the run up the river, recognizing our rig and the American ensign, passing sailors would wave and tap their wrists, amused at our monumental error. Maybe advancing years had something to do with the almost-disastrous mistake.

Shenandoah II was a beautiful boat, but I realized that I was not getting any younger with no one in the family to take over, and I decided to sell. Taking the boat from Raz Parker's yard to Newport where Hank Halsted had opened up shop, I thought the boat would get the proper exposure there, and she did, the sale price netting about 80% of the original investment. Fortunately, that was not the complete end of my sailing career as some of us chartered "White Mist," formerly owned by the Grosvenor family, from Henry Fuller in Baddeck for a run to Newfoundland and then to St. Pierre. Then Stanley Dorman bought a Korean built yawl in Baltimore that provided some of us with happy sailing for a number of years, but then he got tired of the constant maintenance and repair costs and sold out too. Therefore, I have joined the group of former boat owners who mourn the loss of their craft. Also, too, horses that I have ridden and foxhunted on in the past such as Maryland Jim and Skaneatles have gone to the Happy Hunting Ground. Kate, the clever mare that I bought from a neighbor, is now retired from the field and bred to a stallion, standing at Corbett Farm. She is in foal and due to deliver May, 2004, but at the age of 79, I will not be breaking the offspring.

Shenandoah I

Threatening seas

Bob Constable and son, John Igelhart, who is not too happy with the seas running in the Bay of Fundy-1976

Art Gompf, trying to light pipe, on the run up
White Bear Bay

Visitors from the Ramea Islands,
White Bear Bay-1978

Southern coast of Newfoundland

Shenandoah I at St. Pierre

Before the 1982 Bermuda Race
l.to r.- David Westerlund, Art Gompf, F.N. Iglehart,
G. B. Gordon, Henry Pitts, Chris Westerlund, and Paul Swenson

The beginning of a rough trip to Bermuda-1982

St. Thomas after a run from Bermuda
November 1982

St. Maarten-1983

The beach at Anse Marcel
St. Maarten-1983

Swimming hole on Grenada-1984

CHAPTER 34
REUNIONS

My recollections of World War II are recorded in a small book that I wrote entitled "The Short Life of the ASTP" (American Literary Press). Further points of contact with that now distant time is provided annually when Harriet and I join in a reunion with three former members of our unit and their wives. Each one takes a turn in hosting the occasion. The nucleus of the group was formed from four former members of the Army Specialized Training Program (ASTP) assigned to Louisiana State University, their names being picked from a roster alphabetically. All of their last names began with the letter M: Ernest McDaniel, John McCoy, Charles McMurray, and Ralph McGinnis. McDaniel and McCoy were in F Company of my battalion in the 99th Infantry Division. McGinnis was in my Company (G) and McMurray never got overseas having almost died from a case of spinal meningitis incurred in training at Camp Maxey, Texas. About a dozen years ago, partially due to my earlier contacts with McCoy and McDaniel, Harriet and I were invited to join the group for annual reunions in spite of the fact that wc did not qualify alphabetically.

The careers of the others subsequent to the war provide remarkable illustrations of the effect of the GI Bill and the type of abilities taken into the ASTP that only lasted about six months before the program was folded up and the majority of those in it were sent into infantry divisions prior to the Normandy invasion. To qualify for the ASTP, one had to score 10 points or more higher than that required for Officer Candidate School when taking the Army General Classification test at the time of induction. After the war, McDaniel took a lot of courses in Psychology and Anthropology at Columbia and elsewhere, and he was in charge of educational testing for the state of Kentucky for a time and later became a member of the Department of Psychology faculty at Purdue until his retirement. McCoy became a heating engineer, and from the time of Nixon's trip to China, went to the mainland selling and maintaining all types of heating equipment that the Chinese had purchased. In later years, he married a young Chinese woman after the death of his first wife. McGinnis worked for Westinghouse and eventually had four or five patents to his name. He was the first of our group to die. His ashes were interred in a small cemetery at the foothills of the White Mountains in New Hampshire two years ago with the aid of a burial detail assigned from the 10th Mountain Division. McMurray fully recovered from his bout with meningitis and is now very well and hardy. He inherited a specialized poultry business that his family had begun, which is known throughout the country and internationally as well.

Five years ago, it was our turn to play host and we took all eight into our house with the help of cots and roll-away beds. For entertainment, I took them to Corbett Farm to see the horses, to Pimlico Racetrack on the day of the Pimlico Special, and made arrangements for their names to be flashed up on the tote board to welcome them as members of the 99th Division with one of the races being named after the old outfit. We all joined in the presentation of the trophy to the winning owner of that race. On the final day, we concluded matters with a brunch and tour at Ladew Gardens. It was all very pleasant and there was no intimation that McGinnis would be leaving us as soon as he did. I never fully understood Ralph's medical history, but he had gone through polio after the war, as I had, and developed severe complications from a renewal of symptoms of paralysis, difficulty in swallowing, etc. During the war, he had been a lead scout for one of the platoons in my Company. John McCoy, like me, had been a Browning Automatic Rifleman, and Ernest McDaniel was his assistant gunner and ammunition bearer. These annual gatherings are the only reunions that I attend other than an American Veterans Committee (AVC) reunion that we organized at our place last year with about a dozen members of the Baltimore chapter and their wives.

A change has taken place, too, in my law practice as a result of semi-retirement, though there are a few clients whose Wills and Codicils I attend to with an occasional trip to the probate court. Because those clients still remaining are often about my age, it has become necessary to concentrate on various aspects of Elder Law, including the question of eligibility for Medicaid. A great deal of my spare time, of which I have plenty, is devoted to pro bono work for an environmental organization called The Manor Conservancy trying to keep our countryside relatively open and not submerged in mass housing developments by preaching the gospel of tax deductions to be obtained by donating easements on farmland.

It has been a full life and we have been very fortunate in our five children: Hallie has written several books of which *"The Heart of the Goddess"* is the best known; Frank is an audiologist and acting head of the Clark School for the Hearing Impaired; Tom is a computer whiz in Boston; Laney lives quietly tending to the environment in Glencoe; and John has become a commodity specialist for Goldman Sachs, living in England but going to the Middle East, Russia, and other parts of the globe with great frequency. Frank and Karen have a son, Austen, and a daughter, Katy, and Tom's daughter, Jaime, is now a senior at Bard College. I hope that they and others will be interested in these "Recollections."

John McCoy, the author, and Ernest McDaniel
Charleston, West Virginia-1946

CHAPTER 35
HUNT CUP FOLLIES

The last chapter was supposed to be the end of these recollections. However, my severest critic, Harriet, insisted that the tale of my representation of Byron H., arrested for disorderly conduct and other high crimes and misdemeanors after a running of the Maryland Hunt Cup, had to be told.

It happened on a final Saturday in April before Buck Jakes was running in the Hunt Cup. We had gotten home, struggled into our fancy clothes for the Hunt Ball, groaning and swearing at the necessity to place studs in a boiler plate shirt along with cufflinks, when the telephone rang about 7:30 p.m. It was Byron, the grandson of Vera H., an ancient black domestic who worked for our dear friend and neighbor, Jen Voss. Byron, whom his grandmother called "Byroan," had gone to Hereford High School where he was a lacrosse player and was the best friend of Ketch Secor, a near neighbor. Byron tended to move in an all white world and is now married to a striking-looking redhead who is white. The burden of his telephone call was to advise that he had been arrested at a parking area for the Hunt Cup, was innocent of the charges against him, etc.

I asked to talk to the desk sergeant and was informed that Byron would not give them his proper name. That caused me to remonstrate with him on the phone, instructing him to identify himself and I would take it from there.

It was the end of a period of rowdyism among teenagers during and after the running of the most famous steeplechase in America, which had become an extreme headache for the Race Committee and all concerned. There were incidents of a beer bottle being thrown at a horse and rider, a police car overturned, and general acts of vandalism. To put a stop at these depredations, the Race Committee had gotten the State Police to be prepared to shut down what is called Van Hill where the high school lacrosse crowd gathered with the use of sheer numbers of State and County police and attack dogs. When the crowd of beer-drinking, lacrosse players on Van Hill refused to promptly disburse, State and County police moved in in force with nightsticks being freely administered and several legs bitten by dogs.

Byron had gone to the hillside to meet up with friends and claimed that he had done nothing, but had simply been trampled upon by charging police and bitten by one of their dogs. A State trooper was seen videotaping the event.

Though it was a general melee, only three arrests had been made; Byron, and a white couple, who were also charged with possession of marijuana. The cases were to be tried in the District Court in Owings Mills, and I filed a motion to require production and examination of the State Police videotape, which request was granted and a screening held at the State Police headquarters in Pikesville where little was learned due to the ineptness of the cameraman whose shots showed mostly tree branches and the ground, not the encounter between the forces of law and order and the rioters.

The County State's Attorney's office offered a plea bargain: a guilty plea and several hundred hours of community service. Since the marijuana charge involved the white couple, I decided we wanted to get as far away from their case as possible, and filed a motion for severance which was heard by the Honorable Werner Schoeler in the District Court at the time of arraignment.

The entry of a not guilty plea for Byron and the motion for severance seemed to greatly agitate Judge Schoeler, who asked that I come back to his chambers to discuss the matter where he castigated me for not advising my client to accept the plea bargain. When I stood our ground, he went back into court and addressed remarks directly to Byron recommending that in effect he ignore my advice and accept the State's kind offer, which Byron refused to do. Judge Schoeler was so incensed that I thought he would like to hold me in contempt of court.

The upshot was that we entered a prayer for jury trial which I knew would take the matter out of the District Court, bring it to the Circuit Court level where there was a fair chance that the authorities would decide to dismiss the case. This is exactly what happened and Byron "walked."

For a long time, I was *persona non grata* with members of the Race Committee and some of them acted towards yours truly as a member of some fifth column that had infiltrated their ranks. Byron and his attractive wife are now living in Louisville where he has a very good corporate job. His representation was indeed a memorable occasion.